EVENING RITUAL

DAILY CHECKLIST + JOURNAL

CREATED BY EMILY ANNE BRANT

Thank you for purchasing The Ritual Journal!

Just like with our morning journal, there is some work we need to do before you dive into your daily practice. I'll walk you through some prompts to help you work through any limiting beliefs that might be holding you back.

Keep in mind that it takes 30 days to form any new habit, and you may find it difficult to incorporate this and the morning ritual consistently at first. Start with just one, morning OR evening, if it's new to you, and do it for 30 days. Once it's a habit, add the other one. Do another 30 days. It'll soon become second nature, like your morning coffee and breakfast or evening skin care. Remember, if you have 10-20 minutes to scroll your social media feed before bed, you have time to do this.

If you don't have the morning journal: note that each night you'll be prompted to list "5 biggest achievements of my life". These are your goals, to be written as if they've already happened. The evening review will also ask "Did I take action toward my first goal today?" and this refers to the 1 goal you are choosing to focus on first. Do not try to achieve all 5 goals simultaneously.

Congrats on doing this for yourself, and get ready to up-level your entire life! Feel free to keep a blank notepad or journal handy for extra free writing if any of the evening prompts inspire you.

Totally cheering you on,

Emily

LIMITING BELIEFS

I WANT TO ACHIEVE MY GOALS, BUT I HAVE NEGATIVE BELIEFS THAT …
(Examples: I am not educated enough, I don't have enough money or resources, I am not worthy or deserving, I am not beautiful enough, etc…)

I HEAR NEGATIVE VOICES THAT TELL ME…
(Examples: your dreams are too selfish, you can't have it all, you don't have enough time, you will embarrass yourself, etc…)

BUT THE TRUTH IS I AM…
Below, develop a "truth statement" that contradicts all the negative thoughts. Brainstorm positive words that represent the opposite of your feelings above, then craft it into 1-2 sentences. You will write down this statement every day in this journal and say it aloud.

Example: If my limiting beliefs are I am not worthy, not smart enough, not talented enough and I quit everything I start, my truth statement would look something like "I am a worthy, smart, talented, dedicated and passionate woman who is creating her dream life right now and it is my time!" Include "right now" or "now" in your statement.

MY TRUTH STATEMENT:

_____

_____

_____

THE 5 AREAS

Write down the five areas of your life which you would love to improve and be specific on how or what. Examples- Finances- save $50,000, Health- lose 25lbs, Relationships- have a thriving marriage, Mental health- attend 1 social event monthly, Career- achieve top rank in my company, etc.

1

2

3

4

5

MY WHY…

If you've already written this down in the Morning Ritual Journal, write it out again below. If you haven't done this yet- your "why" is the true reason you want to make all the above improvements, and your biggest goals a reality. It must be about you in order to be motivating enough, and it should make you emotional.

5 THINGS I'M GRATEFUL FOR TONIGHT (BE SPECIFIC)

_____

_____

_____

_____

_____

5 BIGGEST ACHIEVEMENTS OF MY LIFE (GOALS)

_____

_____

_____

_____

_____

5 EVALUATION FOR TODAY

DID I TAKE ACTION TOWARD MY FIRST GOAL TODAY, FOCUSED FOR AT LEAST 45 MINS?

_____

DID I KEEP TODAY'S PROMISE TO MYSELF? DID I WORKOUT OR MOVE TODAY?

_____

DID I REPRESENT WHO I AM BECOMING AND WANT TO BE TODAY?

_____

ONE THING I AM PROUD OF MYSELF FOR TODAY:

_____

ONE THING I CAN DO BETTER TOMORROW OR WHERE I CAN SHOW MORE LOVE:

_____

EVENING CHECKLIST

- ☐ CELL PHONE OFF 30 MINS BEFORE SLEEP
- ☐ TAKE 5 DEEP BREATHS
- ☐ 5-10 MINS READING OR JOURNALING
- ☐ SKIN CARE (CLEANSE, TONE, MOISTURIZE, SERUM)
- ☐ ORAL HYGEINE (BRUSH, FLOSS, MOUTHWASH)
- ☐ FULL BODY STRETCH
- ☐ PRAY OR MEDITATE
- ☐ EVENING SUPPLEMENTS OR ESSENTIAL OILS
- ☐ TURN ON DIFFUSER IN BEDROOM WITH CALMING OILS

I FEEL PEACEFUL BECAUSE...

MY TRUTH STATEMENT IS...

MY DREAMS COMING TRUE LOOKS LIKE...
(CLOSE YOUR EYES AND VISUALIZE THIS 2-3 MINUTES, WRITING NOTES HERE IS OPTIONAL)

5 | THINGS I'M GRATEFUL FOR TONIGHT (BE SPECIFIC)

_____

_____

_____

_____

_____

5 | BIGGEST ACHIEVEMENTS OF MY LIFE (GOALS)

_____

_____

_____

_____

_____

5 | EVALUATION FOR TODAY

DID I TAKE ACTION TOWARD MY FIRST GOAL TODAY, FOCUSED FOR AT LEAST 45 MINS?

_____

DID I KEEP TODAY'S PROMISE TO MYSELF? DID I WORKOUT OR MOVE TODAY?

_____

DID I REPRESENT WHO I AM BECOMING AND WANT TO BE TODAY?

_____

ONE THING I AM PROUD OF MYSELF FOR TODAY:

_____

ONE THING I CAN DO BETTER TOMORROW OR WHERE I CAN SHOW MORE LOVE:

_____

EVENING CHECKLIST

- ☐ CELL PHONE OFF 30 MINS BEFORE SLEEP
- ☐ TAKE 5 DEEP BREATHS
- ☐ 5-10 MINS READING OR JOURNALING
- ☐ SKIN CARE (CLEANSE, TONE, MOISTURIZE, SERUM)
- ☐ ORAL HYGEINE (BRUSH, FLOSS, MOUTHWASH)
- ☐ FULL BODY STRETCH
- ☐ PRAY OR MEDITATE
- ☐ EVENING SUPPLEMENTS OR ESSENTIAL OILS
- ☐ TURN ON DIFFUSER IN BEDROOM WITH CALMING OILS

I FEEL PEACEFUL BECAUSE…

MY TRUTH STATEMENT IS…

MY DREAMS COMING TRUE LOOKS LIKE…
(CLOSE YOUR EYES AND VISUALIZE THIS 2-3 MINUTES, WRITING NOTES HERE IS OPTIONAL)

5 | THINGS I'M GRATEFUL FOR TONIGHT (BE SPECIFIC)

_____

_____

_____

_____

_____

5 | BIGGEST ACHIEVEMENTS OF MY LIFE (GOALS)

_____

_____

_____

_____

_____

5 | EVALUATION FOR TODAY

DID I TAKE ACTION TOWARD MY FIRST GOAL TODAY, FOCUSED FOR AT LEAST 45 MINS?

_____

DID I KEEP TODAY'S PROMISE TO MYSELF? DID I WORKOUT OR MOVE TODAY?

_____

DID I REPRESENT WHO I AM BECOMING AND WANT TO BE TODAY?

_____

ONE THING I AM PROUD OF MYSELF FOR TODAY:

_____

ONE THING I CAN DO BETTER TOMORROW OR WHERE I CAN SHOW MORE LOVE:

_____

EVENING CHECKLIST

- ☐ CELL PHONE OFF 30 MINS BEFORE SLEEP
- ☐ TAKE 5 DEEP BREATHS
- ☐ 5-10 MINS READING OR JOURNALING
- ☐ SKIN CARE (CLEANSE, TONE, MOISTURIZE, SERUM)
- ☐ ORAL HYGEINE (BRUSH, FLOSS, MOUTHWASH)
- ☐ FULL BODY STRETCH
- ☐ PRAY OR MEDITATE
- ☐ EVENING SUPPLEMENTS OR ESSENTIAL OILS
- ☐ TURN ON DIFFUSER IN BEDROOM WITH CALMING OILS

I FEEL PEACEFUL BECAUSE…

MY TRUTH STATEMENT IS…

MY DREAMS COMING TRUE LOOKS LIKE…
(CLOSE YOUR EYES AND VISUALIZE THIS 2-3 MINUTES, WRITING NOTES HERE IS OPTIONAL)

5 | THINGS I'M GRATEFUL FOR TONIGHT (BE SPECIFIC)

_____

_____

_____

_____

_____

5 | BIGGEST ACHIEVEMENTS OF MY LIFE (GOALS)

_____

_____

_____

_____

_____

5 | EVALUATION FOR TODAY

DID I TAKE ACTION TOWARD MY FIRST GOAL TODAY, FOCUSED FOR AT LEAST 45 MINS?

_____

DID I KEEP TODAY'S PROMISE TO MYSELF? DID I WORKOUT OR MOVE TODAY?

_____

DID I REPRESENT WHO I AM BECOMING AND WANT TO BE TODAY?

_____

ONE THING I AM PROUD OF MYSELF FOR TODAY:

_____

ONE THING I CAN DO BETTER TOMORROW OR WHERE I CAN SHOW MORE LOVE:

_____

EVENING CHECKLIST

- [ ] CELL PHONE OFF 30 MINS BEFORE SLEEP
- [ ] TAKE 5 DEEP BREATHS
- [ ] 5-10 MINS READING OR JOURNALING
- [ ] SKIN CARE (CLEANSE, TONE, MOISTURIZE, SERUM)
- [ ] ORAL HYGEINE (BRUSH, FLOSS, MOUTHWASH)
- [ ] FULL BODY STRETCH
- [ ] PRAY OR MEDITATE
- [ ] EVENING SUPPLEMENTS OR ESSENTIAL OILS
- [ ] TURN ON DIFFUSER IN BEDROOM WITH CALMING OILS

I FEEL PEACEFUL BECAUSE…

MY TRUTH STATEMENT IS…

MY DREAMS COMING TRUE LOOKS LIKE…
(CLOSE YOUR EYES AND VISUALIZE THIS 2-3 MINUTES, WRITING NOTES HERE IS OPTIONAL)

5 THINGS I'M GRATEFUL FOR TONIGHT (BE SPECIFIC)

5 BIGGEST ACHIEVEMENTS OF MY LIFE (GOALS)

5 EVALUATION FOR TODAY

DID I TAKE ACTION TOWARD MY FIRST GOAL TODAY, FOCUSED FOR AT LEAST 45 MINS?

_____

DID I KEEP TODAY'S PROMISE TO MYSELF? DID I WORKOUT OR MOVE TODAY?

_____

DID I REPRESENT WHO I AM BECOMING AND WANT TO BE TODAY?

_____

ONE THING I AM PROUD OF MYSELF FOR TODAY:

_____

ONE THING I CAN DO BETTER TOMORROW OR WHERE I CAN SHOW MORE LOVE:

_____

EVENING CHECKLIST

- [ ] CELL PHONE OFF 30 MINS BEFORE SLEEP
- [ ] TAKE 5 DEEP BREATHS
- [ ] 5-10 MINS READING OR JOURNALING
- [ ] SKIN CARE (CLEANSE, TONE, MOISTURIZE, SERUM)
- [ ] ORAL HYGEINE (BRUSH, FLOSS, MOUTHWASH)
- [ ] FULL BODY STRETCH
- [ ] PRAY OR MEDITATE
- [ ] EVENING SUPPLEMENTS OR ESSENTIAL OILS
- [ ] TURN ON DIFFUSER IN BEDROOM WITH CALMING OILS

I FEEL PEACEFUL BECAUSE…

MY TRUTH STATEMENT IS…

MY DREAMS COMING TRUE LOOKS LIKE…
(CLOSE YOUR EYES AND VISUALIZE THIS 2-3 MINUTES, WRITING NOTES HERE IS OPTIONAL)

5 THINGS I'M GRATEFUL FOR TONIGHT (BE SPECIFIC)

_____

_____

_____

_____

_____

5 BIGGEST ACHIEVEMENTS OF MY LIFE (GOALS)

_____

_____

_____

_____

_____

5 EVALUATION FOR TODAY

DID I TAKE ACTION TOWARD MY FIRST GOAL TODAY, FOCUSED FOR AT LEAST 45 MINS?

_____

DID I KEEP TODAY'S PROMISE TO MYSELF? DID I WORKOUT OR MOVE TODAY?

_____

DID I REPRESENT WHO I AM BECOMING AND WANT TO BE TODAY?

_____

ONE THING I AM PROUD OF MYSELF FOR TODAY:

_____

ONE THING I CAN DO BETTER TOMORROW OR WHERE I CAN SHOW MORE LOVE:

_____

EVENING CHECKLIST

- ☐ CELL PHONE OFF 30 MINS BEFORE SLEEP
- ☐ TAKE 5 DEEP BREATHS
- ☐ 5-10 MINS READING OR JOURNALING
- ☐ SKIN CARE (CLEANSE, TONE, MOISTURIZE, SERUM)
- ☐ ORAL HYGEINE (BRUSH, FLOSS, MOUTHWASH)
- ☐ FULL BODY STRETCH
- ☐ PRAY OR MEDITATE
- ☐ EVENING SUPPLEMENTS OR ESSENTIAL OILS
- ☐ TURN ON DIFFUSER IN BEDROOM WITH CALMING OILS

I FEEL PEACEFUL BECAUSE…

MY TRUTH STATEMENT IS…

MY DREAMS COMING TRUE LOOKS LIKE…
(CLOSE YOUR EYES AND VISUALIZE THIS 2-3 MINUTES, WRITING NOTES HERE IS OPTIONAL)

5 THINGS I'M GRATEFUL FOR TONIGHT (BE SPECIFIC)

5 BIGGEST ACHIEVEMENTS OF MY LIFE (GOALS)

5 EVALUATION FOR TODAY

DID I TAKE ACTION TOWARD MY FIRST GOAL TODAY, FOCUSED FOR AT LEAST 45 MINS?

_____

DID I KEEP TODAY'S PROMISE TO MYSELF? DID I WORKOUT OR MOVE TODAY?

_____

DID I REPRESENT WHO I AM BECOMING AND WANT TO BE TODAY?

_____

ONE THING I AM PROUD OF MYSELF FOR TODAY:

_____

ONE THING I CAN DO BETTER TOMORROW OR WHERE I CAN SHOW MORE LOVE:

_____

EVENING CHECKLIST

- ☐ CELL PHONE OFF 30 MINS BEFORE SLEEP
- ☐ TAKE 5 DEEP BREATHS
- ☐ 5-10 MINS READING OR JOURNALING
- ☐ SKIN CARE (CLEANSE, TONE, MOISTURIZE, SERUM)
- ☐ ORAL HYGEINE (BRUSH, FLOSS, MOUTHWASH)
- ☐ FULL BODY STRETCH
- ☐ PRAY OR MEDITATE
- ☐ EVENING SUPPLEMENTS OR ESSENTIAL OILS
- ☐ TURN ON DIFFUSER IN BEDROOM WITH CALMING OILS

I FEEL PEACEFUL BECAUSE…

MY TRUTH STATEMENT IS…

MY DREAMS COMING TRUE LOOKS LIKE…
(CLOSE YOUR EYES AND VISUALIZE THIS 2-3 MINUTES, WRITING NOTES HERE IS OPTIONAL)

5 THINGS I'M GRATEFUL FOR TONIGHT (BE SPECIFIC)

_____

_____

_____

_____

_____

5 BIGGEST ACHIEVEMENTS OF MY LIFE (GOALS)

_____

_____

_____

_____

5 EVALUATION FOR TODAY

DID I TAKE ACTION TOWARD MY FIRST GOAL TODAY, FOCUSED FOR AT LEAST 45 MINS?

_____

DID I KEEP TODAY'S PROMISE TO MYSELF? DID I WORKOUT OR MOVE TODAY?

_____

DID I REPRESENT WHO I AM BECOMING AND WANT TO BE TODAY?

_____

ONE THING I AM PROUD OF MYSELF FOR TODAY:

_____

ONE THING I CAN DO BETTER TOMORROW OR WHERE I CAN SHOW MORE LOVE:

_____

EVENING CHECKLIST

- ☐ CELL PHONE OFF 30 MINS BEFORE SLEEP
- ☐ TAKE 5 DEEP BREATHS
- ☐ 5-10 MINS READING OR JOURNALING
- ☐ SKIN CARE (CLEANSE, TONE, MOISTURIZE, SERUM)
- ☐ ORAL HYGEINE (BRUSH, FLOSS, MOUTHWASH)
- ☐ FULL BODY STRETCH
- ☐ PRAY OR MEDITATE
- ☐ EVENING SUPPLEMENTS OR ESSENTIAL OILS
- ☐ TURN ON DIFFUSER IN BEDROOM WITH CALMING OILS

I FEEL PEACEFUL BECAUSE…

MY TRUTH STATEMENT IS…

MY DREAMS COMING TRUE LOOKS LIKE…
(CLOSE YOUR EYES AND VISUALIZE THIS 2-3 MINUTES, WRITING NOTES HERE IS OPTIONAL)

5 | THINGS I'M GRATEFUL FOR TONIGHT (BE SPECIFIC)

_____

_____

_____

_____

_____

5 | BIGGEST ACHIEVEMENTS OF MY LIFE (GOALS)

_____

_____

_____

_____

_____

5 | EVALUATION FOR TODAY

DID I TAKE ACTION TOWARD MY FIRST GOAL TODAY, FOCUSED FOR AT LEAST 45 MINS?

_____

DID I KEEP TODAY'S PROMISE TO MYSELF? DID I WORKOUT OR MOVE TODAY?

_____

DID I REPRESENT WHO I AM BECOMING AND WANT TO BE TODAY?

_____

ONE THING I AM PROUD OF MYSELF FOR TODAY:

_____

ONE THING I CAN DO BETTER TOMORROW OR WHERE I CAN SHOW MORE LOVE:

_____

EVENING CHECKLIST

- ☐ CELL PHONE OFF 30 MINS BEFORE SLEEP
- ☐ TAKE 5 DEEP BREATHS
- ☐ 5-10 MINS READING OR JOURNALING
- ☐ SKIN CARE (CLEANSE, TONE, MOISTURIZE, SERUM)
- ☐ ORAL HYGEINE (BRUSH, FLOSS, MOUTHWASH)
- ☐ FULL BODY STRETCH
- ☐ PRAY OR MEDITATE
- ☐ EVENING SUPPLEMENTS OR ESSENTIAL OILS
- ☐ TURN ON DIFFUSER IN BEDROOM WITH CALMING OILS

I FEEL PEACEFUL BECAUSE…

MY TRUTH STATEMENT IS…

MY DREAMS COMING TRUE LOOKS LIKE…
(CLOSE YOUR EYES AND VISUALIZE THIS 2-3 MINUTES, WRITING NOTES HERE IS OPTIONAL)

5 THINGS I'M GRATEFUL FOR TONIGHT (BE SPECIFIC)

_____

_____

_____

_____

5 BIGGEST ACHIEVEMENTS OF MY LIFE (GOALS)

_____

_____

_____

_____

5 EVALUATION FOR TODAY

DID I TAKE ACTION TOWARD MY FIRST GOAL TODAY, FOCUSED FOR AT LEAST 45 MINS?

_____

DID I KEEP TODAY'S PROMISE TO MYSELF? DID I WORKOUT OR MOVE TODAY?

_____

DID I REPRESENT WHO I AM BECOMING AND WANT TO BE TODAY?

_____

ONE THING I AM PROUD OF MYSELF FOR TODAY:

_____

ONE THING I CAN DO BETTER TOMORROW OR WHERE I CAN SHOW MORE LOVE:

_____

EVENING CHECKLIST

- ☐ CELL PHONE OFF 30 MINS BEFORE SLEEP
- ☐ TAKE 5 DEEP BREATHS
- ☐ 5-10 MINS READING OR JOURNALING
- ☐ SKIN CARE (CLEANSE, TONE, MOISTURIZE, SERUM)
- ☐ ORAL HYGEINE (BRUSH, FLOSS, MOUTHWASH)
- ☐ FULL BODY STRETCH
- ☐ PRAY OR MEDITATE
- ☐ EVENING SUPPLEMENTS OR ESSENTIAL OILS
- ☐ TURN ON DIFFUSER IN BEDROOM WITH CALMING OILS

I FEEL PEACEFUL BECAUSE...

MY TRUTH STATEMENT IS...

MY DREAMS COMING TRUE LOOKS LIKE...
(CLOSE YOUR EYES AND VISUALIZE THIS 2-3 MINUTES, WRITING NOTES HERE IS OPTIONAL)

5 | THINGS I'M GRATEFUL FOR TONIGHT (BE SPECIFIC)

_____

_____

_____

_____

_____

5 | BIGGEST ACHIEVEMENTS OF MY LIFE (GOALS)

_____

_____

_____

_____

_____

5 | EVALUATION FOR TODAY

DID I TAKE ACTION TOWARD MY FIRST GOAL TODAY, FOCUSED FOR AT LEAST 45 MINS?

_____

DID I KEEP TODAY'S PROMISE TO MYSELF? DID I WORKOUT OR MOVE TODAY?

_____

DID I REPRESENT WHO I AM BECOMING AND WANT TO BE TODAY?

_____

ONE THING I AM PROUD OF MYSELF FOR TODAY:

_____

ONE THING I CAN DO BETTER TOMORROW OR WHERE I CAN SHOW MORE LOVE:

_____

EVENING CHECKLIST

- [ ] CELL PHONE OFF 30 MINS BEFORE SLEEP
- [ ] TAKE 5 DEEP BREATHS
- [ ] 5-10 MINS READING OR JOURNALING
- [ ] SKIN CARE (CLEANSE, TONE, MOISTURIZE, SERUM)
- [ ] ORAL HYGEINE (BRUSH, FLOSS, MOUTHWASH)
- [ ] FULL BODY STRETCH
- [ ] PRAY OR MEDITATE
- [ ] EVENING SUPPLEMENTS OR ESSENTIAL OILS
- [ ] TURN ON DIFFUSER IN BEDROOM WITH CALMING OILS

I FEEL PEACEFUL BECAUSE...

MY TRUTH STATEMENT IS...

MY DREAMS COMING TRUE LOOKS LIKE...
(CLOSE YOUR EYES AND VISUALIZE THIS 2-3 MINUTES, WRITING NOTES HERE IS OPTIONAL)

5 | THINGS I'M GRATEFUL FOR TONIGHT (BE SPECIFIC)

_____

_____

_____

_____

_____

5 | BIGGEST ACHIEVEMENTS OF MY LIFE (GOALS)

_____

_____

_____

_____

_____

5 | EVALUATION FOR TODAY

DID I TAKE ACTION TOWARD MY FIRST GOAL TODAY, FOCUSED FOR AT LEAST 45 MINS?

_____

DID I KEEP TODAY'S PROMISE TO MYSELF? DID I WORKOUT OR MOVE TODAY?

_____

DID I REPRESENT WHO I AM BECOMING AND WANT TO BE TODAY?

_____

ONE THING I AM PROUD OF MYSELF FOR TODAY:

_____

ONE THING I CAN DO BETTER TOMORROW OR WHERE I CAN SHOW MORE LOVE:

_____

EVENING CHECKLIST

- [ ] CELL PHONE OFF 30 MINS BEFORE SLEEP
- [ ] TAKE 5 DEEP BREATHS
- [ ] 5-10 MINS READING OR JOURNALING
- [ ] SKIN CARE (CLEANSE, TONE, MOISTURIZE, SERUM)
- [ ] ORAL HYGEINE (BRUSH, FLOSS, MOUTHWASH)
- [ ] FULL BODY STRETCH
- [ ] PRAY OR MEDITATE
- [ ] EVENING SUPPLEMENTS OR ESSENTIAL OILS
- [ ] TURN ON DIFFUSER IN BEDROOM WITH CALMING OILS

I FEEL PEACEFUL BECAUSE...

MY TRUTH STATEMENT IS...

MY DREAMS COMING TRUE LOOKS LIKE...
(CLOSE YOUR EYES AND VISUALIZE THIS 2-3 MINUTES, WRITING NOTES HERE IS OPTIONAL)

5 THINGS I'M GRATEFUL FOR TONIGHT (BE SPECIFIC)

---

5 BIGGEST ACHIEVEMENTS OF MY LIFE (GOALS)

---

5 EVALUATION FOR TODAY

DID I TAKE ACTION TOWARD MY FIRST GOAL TODAY, FOCUSED FOR AT LEAST 45 MINS?

DID I KEEP TODAY'S PROMISE TO MYSELF? DID I WORKOUT OR MOVE TODAY?

DID I REPRESENT WHO I AM BECOMING AND WANT TO BE TODAY?

ONE THING I AM PROUD OF MYSELF FOR TODAY:

ONE THING I CAN DO BETTER TOMORROW OR WHERE I CAN SHOW MORE LOVE:

EVENING CHECKLIST

- ☐ CELL PHONE OFF 30 MINS BEFORE SLEEP
- ☐ TAKE 5 DEEP BREATHS
- ☐ 5-10 MINS READING OR JOURNALING
- ☐ SKIN CARE (CLEANSE, TONE, MOISTURIZE, SERUM)
- ☐ ORAL HYGEINE (BRUSH, FLOSS, MOUTHWASH)
- ☐ FULL BODY STRETCH
- ☐ PRAY OR MEDITATE
- ☐ EVENING SUPPLEMENTS OR ESSENTIAL OILS
- ☐ TURN ON DIFFUSER IN BEDROOM WITH CALMING OILS

I FEEL PEACEFUL BECAUSE…

MY TRUTH STATEMENT IS…

MY DREAMS COMING TRUE LOOKS LIKE…
(CLOSE YOUR EYES AND VISUALIZE THIS 2-3 MINUTES, WRITING NOTES HERE IS OPTIONAL)

5 | THINGS I'M GRATEFUL FOR TONIGHT (BE SPECIFIC)

_____

_____

_____

_____

_____

5 | BIGGEST ACHIEVEMENTS OF MY LIFE (GOALS)

_____

_____

_____

_____

_____

5 | EVALUATION FOR TODAY

DID I TAKE ACTION TOWARD MY FIRST GOAL TODAY, FOCUSED FOR AT LEAST 45 MINS?

_____

DID I KEEP TODAY'S PROMISE TO MYSELF? DID I WORKOUT OR MOVE TODAY?

_____

DID I REPRESENT WHO I AM BECOMING AND WANT TO BE TODAY?

_____

ONE THING I AM PROUD OF MYSELF FOR TODAY:

_____

ONE THING I CAN DO BETTER TOMORROW OR WHERE I CAN SHOW MORE LOVE:

_____

EVENING CHECKLIST

- ☐ CELL PHONE OFF 30 MINS BEFORE SLEEP
- ☐ TAKE 5 DEEP BREATHS
- ☐ 5-10 MINS READING OR JOURNALING
- ☐ SKIN CARE (CLEANSE, TONE, MOISTURIZE, SERUM)
- ☐ ORAL HYGEINE (BRUSH, FLOSS, MOUTHWASH)
- ☐ FULL BODY STRETCH
- ☐ PRAY OR MEDITATE
- ☐ EVENING SUPPLEMENTS OR ESSENTIAL OILS
- ☐ TURN ON DIFFUSER IN BEDROOM WITH CALMING OILS

I FEEL PEACEFUL BECAUSE…

MY TRUTH STATEMENT IS…

MY DREAMS COMING TRUE LOOKS LIKE…
(CLOSE YOUR EYES AND VISUALIZE THIS 2-3 MINUTES, WRITING NOTES HERE IS OPTIONAL)

5 | THINGS I'M GRATEFUL FOR TONIGHT (BE SPECIFIC)

_____

_____

_____

_____

_____

5 | BIGGEST ACHIEVEMENTS OF MY LIFE (GOALS)

_____

_____

_____

_____

_____

5 | EVALUATION FOR TODAY

DID I TAKE ACTION TOWARD MY FIRST GOAL TODAY, FOCUSED FOR AT LEAST 45 MINS?

_____

DID I KEEP TODAY'S PROMISE TO MYSELF? DID I WORKOUT OR MOVE TODAY?

_____

DID I REPRESENT WHO I AM BECOMING AND WANT TO BE TODAY?

_____

ONE THING I AM PROUD OF MYSELF FOR TODAY:

_____

ONE THING I CAN DO BETTER TOMORROW OR WHERE I CAN SHOW MORE LOVE:

_____

EVENING CHECKLIST

- ☐ CELL PHONE OFF 30 MINS BEFORE SLEEP
- ☐ TAKE 5 DEEP BREATHS
- ☐ 5-10 MINS READING OR JOURNALING
- ☐ SKIN CARE (CLEANSE, TONE, MOISTURIZE, SERUM)
- ☐ ORAL HYGEINE (BRUSH, FLOSS, MOUTHWASH)
- ☐ FULL BODY STRETCH
- ☐ PRAY OR MEDITATE
- ☐ EVENING SUPPLEMENTS OR ESSENTIAL OILS
- ☐ TURN ON DIFFUSER IN BEDROOM WITH CALMING OILS

I FEEL PEACEFUL BECAUSE...

MY TRUTH STATEMENT IS...

MY DREAMS COMING TRUE LOOKS LIKE...
(CLOSE YOUR EYES AND VISUALIZE THIS 2-3 MINUTES, WRITING NOTES HERE IS OPTIONAL)

5 THINGS I'M GRATEFUL FOR TONIGHT (BE SPECIFIC)

5 BIGGEST ACHIEVEMENTS OF MY LIFE (GOALS)

_____

_____

_____

_____

_____

_____

_____

_____

_____

_____

5 EVALUATION FOR TODAY

DID I TAKE ACTION TOWARD MY FIRST GOAL TODAY, FOCUSED FOR AT LEAST 45 MINS?

_____

DID I KEEP TODAY'S PROMISE TO MYSELF? DID I WORKOUT OR MOVE TODAY?

_____

DID I REPRESENT WHO I AM BECOMING AND WANT TO BE TODAY?

_____

ONE THING I AM PROUD OF MYSELF FOR TODAY:

_____

ONE THING I CAN DO BETTER TOMORROW OR WHERE I CAN SHOW MORE LOVE:

_____

EVENING CHECKLIST

- [ ] CELL PHONE OFF 30 MINS BEFORE SLEEP
- [ ] TAKE 5 DEEP BREATHS
- [ ] 5-10 MINS READING OR JOURNALING
- [ ] SKIN CARE (CLEANSE, TONE, MOISTURIZE, SERUM)
- [ ] ORAL HYGEINE (BRUSH, FLOSS, MOUTHWASH)
- [ ] FULL BODY STRETCH
- [ ] PRAY OR MEDITATE
- [ ] EVENING SUPPLEMENTS OR ESSENTIAL OILS
- [ ] TURN ON DIFFUSER IN BEDROOM WITH CALMING OILS

I FEEL PEACEFUL BECAUSE…

MY TRUTH STATEMENT IS…

MY DREAMS COMING TRUE LOOKS LIKE…
(CLOSE YOUR EYES AND VISUALIZE THIS 2-3 MINUTES, WRITING NOTES HERE IS OPTIONAL)

5 | THINGS I'M GRATEFUL FOR TONIGHT (BE SPECIFIC)

_____

_____

_____

_____

_____

5 | BIGGEST ACHIEVEMENTS OF MY LIFE (GOALS)

_____

_____

_____

_____

_____

5 | EVALUATION FOR TODAY

DID I TAKE ACTION TOWARD MY FIRST GOAL TODAY, FOCUSED FOR AT LEAST 45 MINS?

_____

DID I KEEP TODAY'S PROMISE TO MYSELF? DID I WORKOUT OR MOVE TODAY?

_____

DID I REPRESENT WHO I AM BECOMING AND WANT TO BE TODAY?

_____

ONE THING I AM PROUD OF MYSELF FOR TODAY:

_____

ONE THING I CAN DO BETTER TOMORROW OR WHERE I CAN SHOW MORE LOVE:

_____

EVENING CHECKLIST

- ☐ CELL PHONE OFF 30 MINS BEFORE SLEEP
- ☐ TAKE 5 DEEP BREATHS
- ☐ 5-10 MINS READING OR JOURNALING
- ☐ SKIN CARE (CLEANSE, TONE, MOISTURIZE, SERUM)
- ☐ ORAL HYGEINE (BRUSH, FLOSS, MOUTHWASH)
- ☐ FULL BODY STRETCH
- ☐ PRAY OR MEDITATE
- ☐ EVENING SUPPLEMENTS OR ESSENTIAL OILS
- ☐ TURN ON DIFFUSER IN BEDROOM WITH CALMING OILS

I FEEL PEACEFUL BECAUSE…

MY TRUTH STATEMENT IS…

MY DREAMS COMING TRUE LOOKS LIKE…
(CLOSE YOUR EYES AND VISUALIZE THIS 2-3 MINUTES, WRITING NOTES HERE IS OPTIONAL)

5 | THINGS I'M GRATEFUL FOR TONIGHT (BE SPECIFIC)

5 | BIGGEST ACHIEVEMENTS OF MY LIFE (GOALS)

_____

_____

_____

_____

_____

5 | EVALUATION FOR TODAY

DID I TAKE ACTION TOWARD MY FIRST GOAL TODAY, FOCUSED FOR AT LEAST 45 MINS?

_____

DID I KEEP TODAY'S PROMISE TO MYSELF? DID I WORKOUT OR MOVE TODAY?

_____

DID I REPRESENT WHO I AM BECOMING AND WANT TO BE TODAY?

_____

ONE THING I AM PROUD OF MYSELF FOR TODAY:

_____

ONE THING I CAN DO BETTER TOMORROW OR WHERE I CAN SHOW MORE LOVE:

_____

EVENING CHECKLIST

- ☐ CELL PHONE OFF 30 MINS BEFORE SLEEP
- ☐ TAKE 5 DEEP BREATHS
- ☐ 5-10 MINS READING OR JOURNALING
- ☐ SKIN CARE (CLEANSE, TONE, MOISTURIZE, SERUM)
- ☐ ORAL HYGEINE (BRUSH, FLOSS, MOUTHWASH)
- ☐ FULL BODY STRETCH
- ☐ PRAY OR MEDITATE
- ☐ EVENING SUPPLEMENTS OR ESSENTIAL OILS
- ☐ TURN ON DIFFUSER IN BEDROOM WITH CALMING OILS

I FEEL PEACEFUL BECAUSE...

MY TRUTH STATEMENT IS...

MY DREAMS COMING TRUE LOOKS LIKE...
(CLOSE YOUR EYES AND VISUALIZE THIS 2-3 MINUTES, WRITING NOTES HERE IS OPTIONAL)

5 THINGS I'M GRATEFUL FOR TONIGHT (BE SPECIFIC)

_____

_____

_____

_____

_____

5 BIGGEST ACHIEVEMENTS OF MY LIFE (GOALS)

_____

_____

_____

_____

_____

5 EVALUATION FOR TODAY

DID I TAKE ACTION TOWARD MY FIRST GOAL TODAY, FOCUSED FOR AT LEAST 45 MINS?

_____

DID I KEEP TODAY'S PROMISE TO MYSELF? DID I WORKOUT OR MOVE TODAY?

_____

DID I REPRESENT WHO I AM BECOMING AND WANT TO BE TODAY?

_____

ONE THING I AM PROUD OF MYSELF FOR TODAY:

_____

ONE THING I CAN DO BETTER TOMORROW OR WHERE I CAN SHOW MORE LOVE:

_____

EVENING CHECKLIST

- [ ] CELL PHONE OFF 30 MINS BEFORE SLEEP
- [ ] TAKE 5 DEEP BREATHS
- [ ] 5-10 MINS READING OR JOURNALING
- [ ] SKIN CARE (CLEANSE, TONE, MOISTURIZE, SERUM)
- [ ] ORAL HYGEINE (BRUSH, FLOSS, MOUTHWASH)
- [ ] FULL BODY STRETCH
- [ ] PRAY OR MEDITATE
- [ ] EVENING SUPPLEMENTS OR ESSENTIAL OILS
- [ ] TURN ON DIFFUSER IN BEDROOM WITH CALMING OILS

I FEEL PEACEFUL BECAUSE...

MY TRUTH STATEMENT IS...

MY DREAMS COMING TRUE LOOKS LIKE...
(CLOSE YOUR EYES AND VISUALIZE THIS 2-3 MINUTES, WRITING NOTES HERE IS OPTIONAL)

5 | THINGS I'M GRATEFUL FOR TONIGHT (BE SPECIFIC)

---

5 | BIGGEST ACHIEVEMENTS OF MY LIFE (GOALS)

---

5 | EVALUATION FOR TODAY

DID I TAKE ACTION TOWARD MY FIRST GOAL TODAY, FOCUSED FOR AT LEAST 45 MINS?

DID I KEEP TODAY'S PROMISE TO MYSELF? DID I WORKOUT OR MOVE TODAY?

DID I REPRESENT WHO I AM BECOMING AND WANT TO BE TODAY?

ONE THING I AM PROUD OF MYSELF FOR TODAY:

ONE THING I CAN DO BETTER TOMORROW OR WHERE I CAN SHOW MORE LOVE:

EVENING CHECKLIST

- ☐ CELL PHONE OFF 30 MINS BEFORE SLEEP

- ☐ TAKE 5 DEEP BREATHS

- ☐ 5-10 MINS READING OR JOURNALING

- ☐ SKIN CARE (CLEANSE, TONE, MOISTURIZE, SERUM)

- ☐ ORAL HYGEINE (BRUSH, FLOSS, MOUTHWASH)

- ☐ FULL BODY STRETCH

- ☐ PRAY OR MEDITATE

- ☐ EVENING SUPPLEMENTS OR ESSENTIAL OILS

- ☐ TURN ON DIFFUSER IN BEDROOM WITH CALMING OILS

I FEEL PEACEFUL BECAUSE…

MY TRUTH STATEMENT IS…

MY DREAMS COMING TRUE LOOKS LIKE…
(CLOSE YOUR EYES AND VISUALIZE THIS 2-3 MINUTES, WRITING NOTES HERE IS OPTIONAL)

5 THINGS I'M GRATEFUL FOR TONIGHT (BE SPECIFIC)

_____

_____

_____

_____

_____

5 BIGGEST ACHIEVEMENTS OF MY LIFE (GOALS)

_____

_____

_____

_____

_____

5 EVALUATION FOR TODAY

DID I TAKE ACTION TOWARD MY FIRST GOAL TODAY, FOCUSED FOR AT LEAST 45 MINS?

_____

DID I KEEP TODAY'S PROMISE TO MYSELF? DID I WORKOUT OR MOVE TODAY?

_____

DID I REPRESENT WHO I AM BECOMING AND WANT TO BE TODAY?

_____

ONE THING I AM PROUD OF MYSELF FOR TODAY:

_____

ONE THING I CAN DO BETTER TOMORROW OR WHERE I CAN SHOW MORE LOVE:

_____

EVENING CHECKLIST

- [ ] CELL PHONE OFF 30 MINS BEFORE SLEEP
- [ ] TAKE 5 DEEP BREATHS
- [ ] 5-10 MINS READING OR JOURNALING
- [ ] SKIN CARE (CLEANSE, TONE, MOISTURIZE, SERUM)
- [ ] ORAL HYGEINE (BRUSH, FLOSS, MOUTHWASH)
- [ ] FULL BODY STRETCH
- [ ] PRAY OR MEDITATE
- [ ] EVENING SUPPLEMENTS OR ESSENTIAL OILS
- [ ] TURN ON DIFFUSER IN BEDROOM WITH CALMING OILS

I FEEL PEACEFUL BECAUSE…

MY TRUTH STATEMENT IS…

MY DREAMS COMING TRUE LOOKS LIKE…
(CLOSE YOUR EYES AND VISUALIZE THIS 2-3 MINUTES, WRITING NOTES HERE IS OPTIONAL)

5 THINGS I'M GRATEFUL FOR TONIGHT (BE SPECIFIC)

_____

_____

_____

_____

_____

5 BIGGEST ACHIEVEMENTS OF MY LIFE (GOALS)

_____

_____

_____

_____

_____

5 EVALUATION FOR TODAY

DID I TAKE ACTION TOWARD MY FIRST GOAL TODAY, FOCUSED FOR AT LEAST 45 MINS?

_____

DID I KEEP TODAY'S PROMISE TO MYSELF? DID I WORKOUT OR MOVE TODAY?

_____

DID I REPRESENT WHO I AM BECOMING AND WANT TO BE TODAY?

_____

ONE THING I AM PROUD OF MYSELF FOR TODAY:

_____

ONE THING I CAN DO BETTER TOMORROW OR WHERE I CAN SHOW MORE LOVE:

_____

EVENING CHECKLIST

- ☐ CELL PHONE OFF 30 MINS BEFORE SLEEP
- ☐ TAKE 5 DEEP BREATHS
- ☐ 5-10 MINS READING OR JOURNALING
- ☐ SKIN CARE (CLEANSE, TONE, MOISTURIZE, SERUM)
- ☐ ORAL HYGEINE (BRUSH, FLOSS, MOUTHWASH)
- ☐ FULL BODY STRETCH
- ☐ PRAY OR MEDITATE
- ☐ EVENING SUPPLEMENTS OR ESSENTIAL OILS
- ☐ TURN ON DIFFUSER IN BEDROOM WITH CALMING OILS

I FEEL PEACEFUL BECAUSE...

MY TRUTH STATEMENT IS...

MY DREAMS COMING TRUE LOOKS LIKE...
(CLOSE YOUR EYES AND VISUALIZE THIS 2-3 MINUTES, WRITING NOTES HERE IS OPTIONAL)

5 THINGS I'M GRATEFUL FOR TONIGHT (BE SPECIFIC)

_____

_____

_____

_____

_____

5 BIGGEST ACHIEVEMENTS OF MY LIFE (GOALS)

_____

_____

_____

_____

_____

5 EVALUATION FOR TODAY

DID I TAKE ACTION TOWARD MY FIRST GOAL TODAY, FOCUSED FOR AT LEAST 45 MINS?

_____

DID I KEEP TODAY'S PROMISE TO MYSELF? DID I WORKOUT OR MOVE TODAY?

_____

DID I REPRESENT WHO I AM BECOMING AND WANT TO BE TODAY?

_____

ONE THING I AM PROUD OF MYSELF FOR TODAY:

_____

ONE THING I CAN DO BETTER TOMORROW OR WHERE I CAN SHOW MORE LOVE:

_____

EVENING CHECKLIST

- [ ] CELL PHONE OFF 30 MINS BEFORE SLEEP
- [ ] TAKE 5 DEEP BREATHS
- [ ] 5-10 MINS READING OR JOURNALING
- [ ] SKIN CARE (CLEANSE, TONE, MOISTURIZE, SERUM)
- [ ] ORAL HYGEINE (BRUSH, FLOSS, MOUTHWASH)
- [ ] FULL BODY STRETCH
- [ ] PRAY OR MEDITATE
- [ ] EVENING SUPPLEMENTS OR ESSENTIAL OILS
- [ ] TURN ON DIFFUSER IN BEDROOM WITH CALMING OILS

I FEEL PEACEFUL BECAUSE...

MY TRUTH STATEMENT IS...

MY DREAMS COMING TRUE LOOKS LIKE...
(CLOSE YOUR EYES AND VISUALIZE THIS 2-3 MINUTES, WRITING NOTES HERE IS OPTIONAL)

5 THINGS I'M GRATEFUL FOR TONIGHT (BE SPECIFIC)

_____

_____

_____

_____

_____

5 BIGGEST ACHIEVEMENTS OF MY LIFE (GOALS)

_____

_____

_____

_____

_____

5 EVALUATION FOR TODAY

DID I TAKE ACTION TOWARD MY FIRST GOAL TODAY, FOCUSED FOR AT LEAST 45 MINS?

_____

DID I KEEP TODAY'S PROMISE TO MYSELF? DID I WORKOUT OR MOVE TODAY?

_____

DID I REPRESENT WHO I AM BECOMING AND WANT TO BE TODAY?

_____

ONE THING I AM PROUD OF MYSELF FOR TODAY:

_____

ONE THING I CAN DO BETTER TOMORROW OR WHERE I CAN SHOW MORE LOVE:

_____

EVENING CHECKLIST

- ☐ CELL PHONE OFF 30 MINS BEFORE SLEEP
- ☐ TAKE 5 DEEP BREATHS
- ☐ 5-10 MINS READING OR JOURNALING
- ☐ SKIN CARE (CLEANSE, TONE, MOISTURIZE, SERUM)
- ☐ ORAL HYGEINE (BRUSH, FLOSS, MOUTHWASH)
- ☐ FULL BODY STRETCH
- ☐ PRAY OR MEDITATE
- ☐ EVENING SUPPLEMENTS OR ESSENTIAL OILS
- ☐ TURN ON DIFFUSER IN BEDROOM WITH CALMING OILS

I FEEL PEACEFUL BECAUSE…

MY TRUTH STATEMENT IS…

MY DREAMS COMING TRUE LOOKS LIKE…
(CLOSE YOUR EYES AND VISUALIZE THIS 2-3 MINUTES, WRITING NOTES HERE IS
OPTIONAL)

5 | THINGS I'M GRATEFUL FOR TONIGHT (BE SPECIFIC)

_____

_____

_____

_____

5 | BIGGEST ACHIEVEMENTS OF MY LIFE (GOALS)

_____

_____

_____

_____

5 | EVALUATION FOR TODAY

DID I TAKE ACTION TOWARD MY FIRST GOAL TODAY, FOCUSED FOR AT LEAST 45 MINS?

_____

DID I KEEP TODAY'S PROMISE TO MYSELF? DID I WORKOUT OR MOVE TODAY?

_____

DID I REPRESENT WHO I AM BECOMING AND WANT TO BE TODAY?

_____

ONE THING I AM PROUD OF MYSELF FOR TODAY:

_____

ONE THING I CAN DO BETTER TOMORROW OR WHERE I CAN SHOW MORE LOVE:

_____

EVENING CHECKLIST

- ☐ CELL PHONE OFF 30 MINS BEFORE SLEEP
- ☐ TAKE 5 DEEP BREATHS
- ☐ 5-10 MINS READING OR JOURNALING
- ☐ SKIN CARE (CLEANSE, TONE, MOISTURIZE, SERUM)
- ☐ ORAL HYGEINE (BRUSH, FLOSS, MOUTHWASH)
- ☐ FULL BODY STRETCH
- ☐ PRAY OR MEDITATE
- ☐ EVENING SUPPLEMENTS OR ESSENTIAL OILS
- ☐ TURN ON DIFFUSER IN BEDROOM WITH CALMING OILS

I FEEL PEACEFUL BECAUSE...

MY TRUTH STATEMENT IS...

MY DREAMS COMING TRUE LOOKS LIKE...
(CLOSE YOUR EYES AND VISUALIZE THIS 2-3 MINUTES, WRITING NOTES HERE IS OPTIONAL)

5 THINGS I'M GRATEFUL FOR TONIGHT (BE SPECIFIC)

5 BIGGEST ACHIEVEMENTS OF MY LIFE (GOALS)

_____

_____

_____

_____

_____

_____

_____

_____

_____

_____

5 EVALUATION FOR TODAY

DID I TAKE ACTION TOWARD MY FIRST GOAL TODAY, FOCUSED FOR AT LEAST 45 MINS?

_____

DID I KEEP TODAY'S PROMISE TO MYSELF? DID I WORKOUT OR MOVE TODAY?

_____

DID I REPRESENT WHO I AM BECOMING AND WANT TO BE TODAY?

_____

ONE THING I AM PROUD OF MYSELF FOR TODAY:

_____

ONE THING I CAN DO BETTER TOMORROW OR WHERE I CAN SHOW MORE LOVE:

_____

EVENING CHECKLIST

- ☐ CELL PHONE OFF 30 MINS BEFORE SLEEP
- ☐ TAKE 5 DEEP BREATHS
- ☐ 5-10 MINS READING OR JOURNALING
- ☐ SKIN CARE (CLEANSE, TONE, MOISTURIZE, SERUM)
- ☐ ORAL HYGEINE (BRUSH, FLOSS, MOUTHWASH)
- ☐ FULL BODY STRETCH
- ☐ PRAY OR MEDITATE
- ☐ EVENING SUPPLEMENTS OR ESSENTIAL OILS
- ☐ TURN ON DIFFUSER IN BEDROOM WITH CALMING OILS

I FEEL PEACEFUL BECAUSE…

MY TRUTH STATEMENT IS…

MY DREAMS COMING TRUE LOOKS LIKE…
(CLOSE YOUR EYES AND VISUALIZE THIS 2-3 MINUTES, WRITING NOTES HERE IS OPTIONAL)

5 | THINGS I'M GRATEFUL FOR TONIGHT (BE SPECIFIC)

5 | BIGGEST ACHIEVEMENTS OF MY LIFE (GOALS)

_____

_____

_____

_____

_____

_____

_____

_____

_____

_____

5 | EVALUATION FOR TODAY

DID I TAKE ACTION TOWARD MY FIRST GOAL TODAY, FOCUSED FOR AT LEAST 45 MINS?

_____

DID I KEEP TODAY'S PROMISE TO MYSELF? DID I WORKOUT OR MOVE TODAY?

_____

DID I REPRESENT WHO I AM BECOMING AND WANT TO BE TODAY?

_____

ONE THING I AM PROUD OF MYSELF FOR TODAY:

_____

ONE THING I CAN DO BETTER TOMORROW OR WHERE I CAN SHOW MORE LOVE:

_____

EVENING CHECKLIST

- ☐ CELL PHONE OFF 30 MINS BEFORE SLEEP
- ☐ TAKE 5 DEEP BREATHS
- ☐ 5-10 MINS READING OR JOURNALING
- ☐ SKIN CARE (CLEANSE, TONE, MOISTURIZE, SERUM)
- ☐ ORAL HYGEINE (BRUSH, FLOSS, MOUTHWASH)
- ☐ FULL BODY STRETCH
- ☐ PRAY OR MEDITATE
- ☐ EVENING SUPPLEMENTS OR ESSENTIAL OILS
- ☐ TURN ON DIFFUSER IN BEDROOM WITH CALMING OILS

I FEEL PEACEFUL BECAUSE…

MY TRUTH STATEMENT IS…

MY DREAMS COMING TRUE LOOKS LIKE…
(CLOSE YOUR EYES AND VISUALIZE THIS 2-3 MINUTES, WRITING NOTES HERE IS OPTIONAL)

5 THINGS I'M GRATEFUL FOR TONIGHT (BE SPECIFIC)

_____

_____

_____

_____

_____

5 BIGGEST ACHIEVEMENTS OF MY LIFE (GOALS)

_____

_____

_____

_____

_____

5 EVALUATION FOR TODAY

DID I TAKE ACTION TOWARD MY FIRST GOAL TODAY, FOCUSED FOR AT LEAST 45 MINS?

_____

DID I KEEP TODAY'S PROMISE TO MYSELF? DID I WORKOUT OR MOVE TODAY?

_____

DID I REPRESENT WHO I AM BECOMING AND WANT TO BE TODAY?

_____

ONE THING I AM PROUD OF MYSELF FOR TODAY:

_____

ONE THING I CAN DO BETTER TOMORROW OR WHERE I CAN SHOW MORE LOVE:

_____

EVENING CHECKLIST

- [ ] CELL PHONE OFF 30 MINS BEFORE SLEEP
- [ ] TAKE 5 DEEP BREATHS
- [ ] 5-10 MINS READING OR JOURNALING
- [ ] SKIN CARE (CLEANSE, TONE, MOISTURIZE, SERUM)
- [ ] ORAL HYGEINE (BRUSH, FLOSS, MOUTHWASH)
- [ ] FULL BODY STRETCH
- [ ] PRAY OR MEDITATE
- [ ] EVENING SUPPLEMENTS OR ESSENTIAL OILS
- [ ] TURN ON DIFFUSER IN BEDROOM WITH CALMING OILS

I FEEL PEACEFUL BECAUSE...

MY TRUTH STATEMENT IS...

MY DREAMS COMING TRUE LOOKS LIKE...
(CLOSE YOUR EYES AND VISUALIZE THIS 2-3 MINUTES, WRITING NOTES HERE IS OPTIONAL)

5 THINGS I'M GRATEFUL FOR TONIGHT (BE SPECIFIC)

_____

_____

_____

_____

_____

5 BIGGEST ACHIEVEMENTS OF MY LIFE (GOALS)

_____

_____

_____

_____

_____

5 EVALUATION FOR TODAY

DID I TAKE ACTION TOWARD MY FIRST GOAL TODAY, FOCUSED FOR AT LEAST 45 MINS?

_____

DID I KEEP TODAY'S PROMISE TO MYSELF? DID I WORKOUT OR MOVE TODAY?

_____

DID I REPRESENT WHO I AM BECOMING AND WANT TO BE TODAY?

_____

ONE THING I AM PROUD OF MYSELF FOR TODAY:

_____

ONE THING I CAN DO BETTER TOMORROW OR WHERE I CAN SHOW MORE LOVE:

_____

EVENING CHECKLIST

- ☐ CELL PHONE OFF 30 MINS BEFORE SLEEP
- ☐ TAKE 5 DEEP BREATHS
- ☐ 5-10 MINS READING OR JOURNALING
- ☐ SKIN CARE (CLEANSE, TONE, MOISTURIZE, SERUM)
- ☐ ORAL HYGEINE (BRUSH, FLOSS, MOUTHWASH)
- ☐ FULL BODY STRETCH
- ☐ PRAY OR MEDITATE
- ☐ EVENING SUPPLEMENTS OR ESSENTIAL OILS
- ☐ TURN ON DIFFUSER IN BEDROOM WITH CALMING OILS

I FEEL PEACEFUL BECAUSE…

MY TRUTH STATEMENT IS…

MY DREAMS COMING TRUE LOOKS LIKE…
(CLOSE YOUR EYES AND VISUALIZE THIS 2-3 MINUTES, WRITING NOTES HERE IS OPTIONAL)

5 THINGS I'M GRATEFUL FOR TONIGHT (BE SPECIFIC)

5 BIGGEST ACHIEVEMENTS OF MY LIFE (GOALS)

_____

_____

_____

_____

_____

_____

_____

_____

_____

_____

5 EVALUATION FOR TODAY

DID I TAKE ACTION TOWARD MY FIRST GOAL TODAY, FOCUSED FOR AT LEAST 45 MINS?

_____

DID I KEEP TODAY'S PROMISE TO MYSELF? DID I WORKOUT OR MOVE TODAY?

_____

DID I REPRESENT WHO I AM BECOMING AND WANT TO BE TODAY?

_____

ONE THING I AM PROUD OF MYSELF FOR TODAY:

_____

ONE THING I CAN DO BETTER TOMORROW OR WHERE I CAN SHOW MORE LOVE:

_____

EVENING CHECKLIST

- ☐ CELL PHONE OFF 30 MINS BEFORE SLEEP

- ☐ TAKE 5 DEEP BREATHS

- ☐ 5-10 MINS READING OR JOURNALING

- ☐ SKIN CARE (CLEANSE, TONE, MOISTURIZE, SERUM)

- ☐ ORAL HYGEINE (BRUSH, FLOSS, MOUTHWASH)

- ☐ FULL BODY STRETCH

- ☐ PRAY OR MEDITATE

- ☐ EVENING SUPPLEMENTS OR ESSENTIAL OILS

- ☐ TURN ON DIFFUSER IN BEDROOM WITH CALMING OILS

I FEEL PEACEFUL BECAUSE...

MY TRUTH STATEMENT IS...

MY DREAMS COMING TRUE LOOKS LIKE...
(CLOSE YOUR EYES AND VISUALIZE THIS 2-3 MINUTES, WRITING NOTES HERE IS
OPTIONAL)

5 THINGS I'M GRATEFUL FOR TONIGHT (BE SPECIFIC)

_____

_____

_____

_____

_____

5 BIGGEST ACHIEVEMENTS OF MY LIFE (GOALS)

_____

_____

_____

_____

_____

5 EVALUATION FOR TODAY

DID I TAKE ACTION TOWARD MY FIRST GOAL TODAY, FOCUSED FOR AT LEAST 45 MINS?

_____

DID I KEEP TODAY'S PROMISE TO MYSELF? DID I WORKOUT OR MOVE TODAY?

_____

DID I REPRESENT WHO I AM BECOMING AND WANT TO BE TODAY?

_____

ONE THING I AM PROUD OF MYSELF FOR TODAY:

_____

ONE THING I CAN DO BETTER TOMORROW OR WHERE I CAN SHOW MORE LOVE:

_____

EVENING CHECKLIST

- ☐ CELL PHONE OFF 30 MINS BEFORE SLEEP
- ☐ TAKE 5 DEEP BREATHS
- ☐ 5-10 MINS READING OR JOURNALING
- ☐ SKIN CARE (CLEANSE, TONE, MOISTURIZE, SERUM)
- ☐ ORAL HYGEINE (BRUSH, FLOSS, MOUTHWASH)
- ☐ FULL BODY STRETCH
- ☐ PRAY OR MEDITATE
- ☐ EVENING SUPPLEMENTS OR ESSENTIAL OILS
- ☐ TURN ON DIFFUSER IN BEDROOM WITH CALMING OILS

I FEEL PEACEFUL BECAUSE…

MY TRUTH STATEMENT IS…

MY DREAMS COMING TRUE LOOKS LIKE…
(CLOSE YOUR EYES AND VISUALIZE THIS 2-3 MINUTES, WRITING NOTES HERE IS OPTIONAL)

5 THINGS I'M GRATEFUL FOR TONIGHT (BE SPECIFIC)

_____

_____

_____

_____

_____

5 BIGGEST ACHIEVEMENTS OF MY LIFE (GOALS)

_____

_____

_____

_____

5 EVALUATION FOR TODAY

DID I TAKE ACTION TOWARD MY FIRST GOAL TODAY, FOCUSED FOR AT LEAST 45 MINS?

_____

DID I KEEP TODAY'S PROMISE TO MYSELF? DID I WORKOUT OR MOVE TODAY?

_____

DID I REPRESENT WHO I AM BECOMING AND WANT TO BE TODAY?

_____

ONE THING I AM PROUD OF MYSELF FOR TODAY:

_____

ONE THING I CAN DO BETTER TOMORROW OR WHERE I CAN SHOW MORE LOVE:

_____

EVENING CHECKLIST

- ☐ CELL PHONE OFF 30 MINS BEFORE SLEEP
- ☐ TAKE 5 DEEP BREATHS
- ☐ 5-10 MINS READING OR JOURNALING
- ☐ SKIN CARE (CLEANSE, TONE, MOISTURIZE, SERUM)
- ☐ ORAL HYGEINE (BRUSH, FLOSS, MOUTHWASH)
- ☐ FULL BODY STRETCH
- ☐ PRAY OR MEDITATE
- ☐ EVENING SUPPLEMENTS OR ESSENTIAL OILS
- ☐ TURN ON DIFFUSER IN BEDROOM WITH CALMING OILS

I FEEL PEACEFUL BECAUSE…

MY TRUTH STATEMENT IS…

MY DREAMS COMING TRUE LOOKS LIKE…
(CLOSE YOUR EYES AND VISUALIZE THIS 2-3 MINUTES, WRITING NOTES HERE IS OPTIONAL)

5 | THINGS I'M GRATEFUL FOR TONIGHT (BE SPECIFIC)

_____

_____

_____

_____

_____

5 | BIGGEST ACHIEVEMENTS OF MY LIFE (GOALS)

_____

_____

_____

_____

5 | EVALUATION FOR TODAY

DID I TAKE ACTION TOWARD MY FIRST GOAL TODAY, FOCUSED FOR AT LEAST 45 MINS?

_____

DID I KEEP TODAY'S PROMISE TO MYSELF? DID I WORKOUT OR MOVE TODAY?

_____

DID I REPRESENT WHO I AM BECOMING AND WANT TO BE TODAY?

_____

ONE THING I AM PROUD OF MYSELF FOR TODAY:

_____

ONE THING I CAN DO BETTER TOMORROW OR WHERE I CAN SHOW MORE LOVE:

_____

EVENING CHECKLIST

- ☐ CELL PHONE OFF 30 MINS BEFORE SLEEP
- ☐ TAKE 5 DEEP BREATHS
- ☐ 5-10 MINS READING OR JOURNALING
- ☐ SKIN CARE (CLEANSE, TONE, MOISTURIZE, SERUM)
- ☐ ORAL HYGEINE (BRUSH, FLOSS, MOUTHWASH)
- ☐ FULL BODY STRETCH
- ☐ PRAY OR MEDITATE
- ☐ EVENING SUPPLEMENTS OR ESSENTIAL OILS
- ☐ TURN ON DIFFUSER IN BEDROOM WITH CALMING OILS

I FEEL PEACEFUL BECAUSE…

MY TRUTH STATEMENT IS…

MY DREAMS COMING TRUE LOOKS LIKE…
(CLOSE YOUR EYES AND VISUALIZE THIS 2-3 MINUTES, WRITING NOTES HERE IS OPTIONAL)

5 THINGS I'M GRATEFUL FOR TONIGHT (BE SPECIFIC)

_____

_____

_____

_____

_____

5 BIGGEST ACHIEVEMENTS OF MY LIFE (GOALS)

_____

_____

_____

_____

_____

5 EVALUATION FOR TODAY

DID I TAKE ACTION TOWARD MY FIRST GOAL TODAY, FOCUSED FOR AT LEAST 45 MINS?

_____

DID I KEEP TODAY'S PROMISE TO MYSELF? DID I WORKOUT OR MOVE TODAY?

_____

DID I REPRESENT WHO I AM BECOMING AND WANT TO BE TODAY?

_____

ONE THING I AM PROUD OF MYSELF FOR TODAY:

_____

ONE THING I CAN DO BETTER TOMORROW OR WHERE I CAN SHOW MORE LOVE:

_____

EVENING CHECKLIST

- [ ] CELL PHONE OFF 30 MINS BEFORE SLEEP
- [ ] TAKE 5 DEEP BREATHS
- [ ] 5-10 MINS READING OR JOURNALING
- [ ] SKIN CARE (CLEANSE, TONE, MOISTURIZE, SERUM)
- [ ] ORAL HYGEINE (BRUSH, FLOSS, MOUTHWASH)
- [ ] FULL BODY STRETCH
- [ ] PRAY OR MEDITATE
- [ ] EVENING SUPPLEMENTS OR ESSENTIAL OILS
- [ ] TURN ON DIFFUSER IN BEDROOM WITH CALMING OILS

I FEEL PEACEFUL BECAUSE...

MY TRUTH STATEMENT IS...

MY DREAMS COMING TRUE LOOKS LIKE...
(CLOSE YOUR EYES AND VISUALIZE THIS 2-3 MINUTES, WRITING NOTES HERE IS OPTIONAL)

5 THINGS I'M GRATEFUL FOR TONIGHT (BE SPECIFIC)

_____

_____

_____

_____

_____

5 BIGGEST ACHIEVEMENTS OF MY LIFE (GOALS)

_____

_____

_____

_____

_____

5 EVALUATION FOR TODAY

DID I TAKE ACTION TOWARD MY FIRST GOAL TODAY, FOCUSED FOR AT LEAST 45 MINS?

_____

DID I KEEP TODAY'S PROMISE TO MYSELF? DID I WORKOUT OR MOVE TODAY?

_____

DID I REPRESENT WHO I AM BECOMING AND WANT TO BE TODAY?

_____

ONE THING I AM PROUD OF MYSELF FOR TODAY:

_____

ONE THING I CAN DO BETTER TOMORROW OR WHERE I CAN SHOW MORE LOVE:

_____

EVENING CHECKLIST

- ☐ CELL PHONE OFF 30 MINS BEFORE SLEEP
- ☐ TAKE 5 DEEP BREATHS
- ☐ 5-10 MINS READING OR JOURNALING
- ☐ SKIN CARE (CLEANSE, TONE, MOISTURIZE, SERUM)
- ☐ ORAL HYGEINE (BRUSH, FLOSS, MOUTHWASH)
- ☐ FULL BODY STRETCH
- ☐ PRAY OR MEDITATE
- ☐ EVENING SUPPLEMENTS OR ESSENTIAL OILS
- ☐ TURN ON DIFFUSER IN BEDROOM WITH CALMING OILS

I FEEL PEACEFUL BECAUSE…

MY TRUTH STATEMENT IS…

MY DREAMS COMING TRUE LOOKS LIKE…
(CLOSE YOUR EYES AND VISUALIZE THIS 2-3 MINUTES, WRITING NOTES HERE IS OPTIONAL)

5 | THINGS I'M GRATEFUL FOR TONIGHT (BE SPECIFIC)

_____

_____

_____

_____

_____

5 | BIGGEST ACHIEVEMENTS OF MY LIFE (GOALS)

_____

_____

_____

_____

_____

5 | EVALUATION FOR TODAY

DID I TAKE ACTION TOWARD MY FIRST GOAL TODAY, FOCUSED FOR AT LEAST 45 MINS?

_____

DID I KEEP TODAY'S PROMISE TO MYSELF? DID I WORKOUT OR MOVE TODAY?

_____

DID I REPRESENT WHO I AM BECOMING AND WANT TO BE TODAY?

_____

ONE THING I AM PROUD OF MYSELF FOR TODAY:

_____

ONE THING I CAN DO BETTER TOMORROW OR WHERE I CAN SHOW MORE LOVE:

_____

EVENING CHECKLIST

- ☐ CELL PHONE OFF 30 MINS BEFORE SLEEP
- ☐ TAKE 5 DEEP BREATHS
- ☐ 5-10 MINS READING OR JOURNALING
- ☐ SKIN CARE (CLEANSE, TONE, MOISTURIZE, SERUM)
- ☐ ORAL HYGEINE (BRUSH, FLOSS, MOUTHWASH)
- ☐ FULL BODY STRETCH
- ☐ PRAY OR MEDITATE
- ☐ EVENING SUPPLEMENTS OR ESSENTIAL OILS
- ☐ TURN ON DIFFUSER IN BEDROOM WITH CALMING OILS

I FEEL PEACEFUL BECAUSE…

MY TRUTH STATEMENT IS…

MY DREAMS COMING TRUE LOOKS LIKE…
(CLOSE YOUR EYES AND VISUALIZE THIS 2-3 MINUTES, WRITING NOTES HERE IS OPTIONAL)

5 THINGS I'M GRATEFUL FOR TONIGHT (BE SPECIFIC)

_____

_____

_____

_____

_____

5 BIGGEST ACHIEVEMENTS OF MY LIFE (GOALS)

_____

_____

_____

_____

_____

5 EVALUATION FOR TODAY

DID I TAKE ACTION TOWARD MY FIRST GOAL TODAY, FOCUSED FOR AT LEAST 45 MINS?

_____

DID I KEEP TODAY'S PROMISE TO MYSELF? DID I WORKOUT OR MOVE TODAY?

_____

DID I REPRESENT WHO I AM BECOMING AND WANT TO BE TODAY?

_____

ONE THING I AM PROUD OF MYSELF FOR TODAY:

_____

ONE THING I CAN DO BETTER TOMORROW OR WHERE I CAN SHOW MORE LOVE:

_____

EVENING CHECKLIST

- ☐ CELL PHONE OFF 30 MINS BEFORE SLEEP
- ☐ TAKE 5 DEEP BREATHS
- ☐ 5-10 MINS READING OR JOURNALING
- ☐ SKIN CARE (CLEANSE, TONE, MOISTURIZE, SERUM)
- ☐ ORAL HYGEINE (BRUSH, FLOSS, MOUTHWASH)
- ☐ FULL BODY STRETCH
- ☐ PRAY OR MEDITATE
- ☐ EVENING SUPPLEMENTS OR ESSENTIAL OILS
- ☐ TURN ON DIFFUSER IN BEDROOM WITH CALMING OILS

I FEEL PEACEFUL BECAUSE…

MY TRUTH STATEMENT IS…

MY DREAMS COMING TRUE LOOKS LIKE…
(CLOSE YOUR EYES AND VISUALIZE THIS 2-3 MINUTES, WRITING NOTES HERE IS OPTIONAL)

5 THINGS I'M GRATEFUL FOR TONIGHT (BE SPECIFIC)

_____

_____

_____

_____

_____

5 BIGGEST ACHIEVEMENTS OF MY LIFE (GOALS)

_____

_____

_____

_____

_____

5 EVALUATION FOR TODAY

DID I TAKE ACTION TOWARD MY FIRST GOAL TODAY, FOCUSED FOR AT LEAST 45 MINS?

_____

DID I KEEP TODAY'S PROMISE TO MYSELF? DID I WORKOUT OR MOVE TODAY?

_____

DID I REPRESENT WHO I AM BECOMING AND WANT TO BE TODAY?

_____

ONE THING I AM PROUD OF MYSELF FOR TODAY:

_____

ONE THING I CAN DO BETTER TOMORROW OR WHERE I CAN SHOW MORE LOVE:

_____

EVENING CHECKLIST

- [ ] CELL PHONE OFF 30 MINS BEFORE SLEEP
- [ ] TAKE 5 DEEP BREATHS
- [ ] 5-10 MINS READING OR JOURNALING
- [ ] SKIN CARE (CLEANSE, TONE, MOISTURIZE, SERUM)
- [ ] ORAL HYGEINE (BRUSH, FLOSS, MOUTHWASH)
- [ ] FULL BODY STRETCH
- [ ] PRAY OR MEDITATE
- [ ] EVENING SUPPLEMENTS OR ESSENTIAL OILS
- [ ] TURN ON DIFFUSER IN BEDROOM WITH CALMING OILS

I FEEL PEACEFUL BECAUSE...

MY TRUTH STATEMENT IS...

MY DREAMS COMING TRUE LOOKS LIKE...
(CLOSE YOUR EYES AND VISUALIZE THIS 2-3 MINUTES, WRITING NOTES HERE IS OPTIONAL)

5 | THINGS I'M GRATEFUL FOR TONIGHT (BE SPECIFIC)

5 | BIGGEST ACHIEVEMENTS OF MY LIFE (GOALS)

5 | EVALUATION FOR TODAY

DID I TAKE ACTION TOWARD MY FIRST GOAL TODAY, FOCUSED FOR AT LEAST 45 MINS?

_____

DID I KEEP TODAY'S PROMISE TO MYSELF? DID I WORKOUT OR MOVE TODAY?

_____

DID I REPRESENT WHO I AM BECOMING AND WANT TO BE TODAY?

_____

ONE THING I AM PROUD OF MYSELF FOR TODAY:

_____

ONE THING I CAN DO BETTER TOMORROW OR WHERE I CAN SHOW MORE LOVE:

_____

EVENING CHECKLIST

- ☐ CELL PHONE OFF 30 MINS BEFORE SLEEP
- ☐ TAKE 5 DEEP BREATHS
- ☐ 5-10 MINS READING OR JOURNALING
- ☐ SKIN CARE (CLEANSE, TONE, MOISTURIZE, SERUM)
- ☐ ORAL HYGEINE (BRUSH, FLOSS, MOUTHWASH)
- ☐ FULL BODY STRETCH
- ☐ PRAY OR MEDITATE
- ☐ EVENING SUPPLEMENTS OR ESSENTIAL OILS
- ☐ TURN ON DIFFUSER IN BEDROOM WITH CALMING OILS

I FEEL PEACEFUL BECAUSE…

MY TRUTH STATEMENT IS…

MY DREAMS COMING TRUE LOOKS LIKE…
(CLOSE YOUR EYES AND VISUALIZE THIS 2-3 MINUTES, WRITING NOTES HERE IS OPTIONAL)

5 THINGS I'M GRATEFUL FOR TONIGHT (BE SPECIFIC)	**5** BIGGEST ACHIEVEMENTS OF MY LIFE (GOALS)
_____	_____
_____	_____
_____	_____
_____	_____
_____	_____

5 EVALUATION FOR TODAY

DID I TAKE ACTION TOWARD MY FIRST GOAL TODAY, FOCUSED FOR AT LEAST 45 MINS?

_____

DID I KEEP TODAY'S PROMISE TO MYSELF? DID I WORKOUT OR MOVE TODAY?

_____

DID I REPRESENT WHO I AM BECOMING AND WANT TO BE TODAY?

_____

ONE THING I AM PROUD OF MYSELF FOR TODAY:

_____

ONE THING I CAN DO BETTER TOMORROW OR WHERE I CAN SHOW MORE LOVE:

_____

EVENING CHECKLIST

- ☐ CELL PHONE OFF 30 MINS BEFORE SLEEP
- ☐ TAKE 5 DEEP BREATHS
- ☐ 5-10 MINS READING OR JOURNALING
- ☐ SKIN CARE (CLEANSE, TONE, MOISTURIZE, SERUM)
- ☐ ORAL HYGEINE (BRUSH, FLOSS, MOUTHWASH)
- ☐ FULL BODY STRETCH
- ☐ PRAY OR MEDITATE
- ☐ EVENING SUPPLEMENTS OR ESSENTIAL OILS
- ☐ TURN ON DIFFUSER IN BEDROOM WITH CALMING OILS

I FEEL PEACEFUL BECAUSE…

MY TRUTH STATEMENT IS…

MY DREAMS COMING TRUE LOOKS LIKE…
(CLOSE YOUR EYES AND VISUALIZE THIS 2-3 MINUTES, WRITING NOTES HERE IS OPTIONAL)

5 THINGS I'M GRATEFUL FOR TONIGHT (BE SPECIFIC)

5 BIGGEST ACHIEVEMENTS OF MY LIFE (GOALS)

5 EVALUATION FOR TODAY

DID I TAKE ACTION TOWARD MY FIRST GOAL TODAY, FOCUSED FOR AT LEAST 45 MINS?

_____

DID I KEEP TODAY'S PROMISE TO MYSELF? DID I WORKOUT OR MOVE TODAY?

_____

DID I REPRESENT WHO I AM BECOMING AND WANT TO BE TODAY?

_____

ONE THING I AM PROUD OF MYSELF FOR TODAY:

_____

ONE THING I CAN DO BETTER TOMORROW OR WHERE I CAN SHOW MORE LOVE:

_____

EVENING CHECKLIST

- [ ] CELL PHONE OFF 30 MINS BEFORE SLEEP
- [ ] TAKE 5 DEEP BREATHS
- [ ] 5-10 MINS READING OR JOURNALING
- [ ] SKIN CARE (CLEANSE, TONE, MOISTURIZE, SERUM)
- [ ] ORAL HYGEINE (BRUSH, FLOSS, MOUTHWASH)
- [ ] FULL BODY STRETCH
- [ ] PRAY OR MEDITATE
- [ ] EVENING SUPPLEMENTS OR ESSENTIAL OILS
- [ ] TURN ON DIFFUSER IN BEDROOM WITH CALMING OILS

I FEEL PEACEFUL BECAUSE…

MY TRUTH STATEMENT IS…

MY DREAMS COMING TRUE LOOKS LIKE…
(CLOSE YOUR EYES AND VISUALIZE THIS 2-3 MINUTES, WRITING NOTES HERE IS OPTIONAL)

5 THINGS I'M GRATEFUL FOR TONIGHT (BE SPECIFIC)

_____

_____

_____

_____

_____

5 BIGGEST ACHIEVEMENTS OF MY LIFE (GOALS)

_____

_____

_____

_____

_____

5 EVALUATION FOR TODAY

DID I TAKE ACTION TOWARD MY FIRST GOAL TODAY, FOCUSED FOR AT LEAST 45 MINS?

_____

DID I KEEP TODAY'S PROMISE TO MYSELF? DID I WORKOUT OR MOVE TODAY?

_____

DID I REPRESENT WHO I AM BECOMING AND WANT TO BE TODAY?

_____

ONE THING I AM PROUD OF MYSELF FOR TODAY:

_____

ONE THING I CAN DO BETTER TOMORROW OR WHERE I CAN SHOW MORE LOVE:

_____

EVENING CHECKLIST

- ☐ CELL PHONE OFF 30 MINS BEFORE SLEEP
- ☐ TAKE 5 DEEP BREATHS
- ☐ 5-10 MINS READING OR JOURNALING
- ☐ SKIN CARE (CLEANSE, TONE, MOISTURIZE, SERUM)
- ☐ ORAL HYGEINE (BRUSH, FLOSS, MOUTHWASH)
- ☐ FULL BODY STRETCH
- ☐ PRAY OR MEDITATE
- ☐ EVENING SUPPLEMENTS OR ESSENTIAL OILS
- ☐ TURN ON DIFFUSER IN BEDROOM WITH CALMING OILS

I FEEL PEACEFUL BECAUSE...

MY TRUTH STATEMENT IS...

MY DREAMS COMING TRUE LOOKS LIKE...
(CLOSE YOUR EYES AND VISUALIZE THIS 2-3 MINUTES, WRITING NOTES HERE IS OPTIONAL)

5 THINGS I'M GRATEFUL FOR TONIGHT (BE SPECIFIC)

_____

_____

_____

_____

_____

5 BIGGEST ACHIEVEMENTS OF MY LIFE (GOALS)

_____

_____

_____

_____

_____

5 EVALUATION FOR TODAY

DID I TAKE ACTION TOWARD MY FIRST GOAL TODAY, FOCUSED FOR AT LEAST 45 MINS?

_____

DID I KEEP TODAY'S PROMISE TO MYSELF? DID I WORKOUT OR MOVE TODAY?

_____

DID I REPRESENT WHO I AM BECOMING AND WANT TO BE TODAY?

_____

ONE THING I AM PROUD OF MYSELF FOR TODAY:

_____

ONE THING I CAN DO BETTER TOMORROW OR WHERE I CAN SHOW MORE LOVE:

_____

EVENING CHECKLIST

- ☐ CELL PHONE OFF 30 MINS BEFORE SLEEP
- ☐ TAKE 5 DEEP BREATHS
- ☐ 5-10 MINS READING OR JOURNALING
- ☐ SKIN CARE (CLEANSE, TONE, MOISTURIZE, SERUM)
- ☐ ORAL HYGEINE (BRUSH, FLOSS, MOUTHWASH)
- ☐ FULL BODY STRETCH
- ☐ PRAY OR MEDITATE
- ☐ EVENING SUPPLEMENTS OR ESSENTIAL OILS
- ☐ TURN ON DIFFUSER IN BEDROOM WITH CALMING OILS

I FEEL PEACEFUL BECAUSE…

MY TRUTH STATEMENT IS…

MY DREAMS COMING TRUE LOOKS LIKE…
(CLOSE YOUR EYES AND VISUALIZE THIS 2-3 MINUTES, WRITING NOTES HERE IS OPTIONAL)

5 THINGS I'M GRATEFUL FOR TONIGHT (BE SPECIFIC)

_____

_____

_____

_____

_____

5 BIGGEST ACHIEVEMENTS OF MY LIFE (GOALS)

_____

_____

_____

_____

_____

5 EVALUATION FOR TODAY

DID I TAKE ACTION TOWARD MY FIRST GOAL TODAY, FOCUSED FOR AT LEAST 45 MINS?

_____

DID I KEEP TODAY'S PROMISE TO MYSELF? DID I WORKOUT OR MOVE TODAY?

_____

DID I REPRESENT WHO I AM BECOMING AND WANT TO BE TODAY?

_____

ONE THING I AM PROUD OF MYSELF FOR TODAY:

_____

ONE THING I CAN DO BETTER TOMORROW OR WHERE I CAN SHOW MORE LOVE:

_____

EVENING CHECKLIST

- ☐ CELL PHONE OFF 30 MINS BEFORE SLEEP
- ☐ TAKE 5 DEEP BREATHS
- ☐ 5-10 MINS READING OR JOURNALING
- ☐ SKIN CARE (CLEANSE, TONE, MOISTURIZE, SERUM)
- ☐ ORAL HYGEINE (BRUSH, FLOSS, MOUTHWASH)
- ☐ FULL BODY STRETCH
- ☐ PRAY OR MEDITATE
- ☐ EVENING SUPPLEMENTS OR ESSENTIAL OILS
- ☐ TURN ON DIFFUSER IN BEDROOM WITH CALMING OILS

I FEEL PEACEFUL BECAUSE…

MY TRUTH STATEMENT IS…

MY DREAMS COMING TRUE LOOKS LIKE…
(CLOSE YOUR EYES AND VISUALIZE THIS 2-3 MINUTES, WRITING NOTES HERE IS OPTIONAL)

5 THINGS I'M GRATEFUL FOR TONIGHT (BE SPECIFIC)

_____

_____

_____

_____

_____

5 BIGGEST ACHIEVEMENTS OF MY LIFE (GOALS)

_____

_____

_____

_____

_____

5 EVALUATION FOR TODAY

DID I TAKE ACTION TOWARD MY FIRST GOAL TODAY, FOCUSED FOR AT LEAST 45 MINS?

_____

DID I KEEP TODAY'S PROMISE TO MYSELF? DID I WORKOUT OR MOVE TODAY?

_____

DID I REPRESENT WHO I AM BECOMING AND WANT TO BE TODAY?

_____

ONE THING I AM PROUD OF MYSELF FOR TODAY:

_____

ONE THING I CAN DO BETTER TOMORROW OR WHERE I CAN SHOW MORE LOVE:

_____

EVENING CHECKLIST

- [ ] CELL PHONE OFF 30 MINS BEFORE SLEEP
- [ ] TAKE 5 DEEP BREATHS
- [ ] 5-10 MINS READING OR JOURNALING
- [ ] SKIN CARE (CLEANSE, TONE, MOISTURIZE, SERUM)
- [ ] ORAL HYGEINE (BRUSH, FLOSS, MOUTHWASH)
- [ ] FULL BODY STRETCH
- [ ] PRAY OR MEDITATE
- [ ] EVENING SUPPLEMENTS OR ESSENTIAL OILS
- [ ] TURN ON DIFFUSER IN BEDROOM WITH CALMING OILS

I FEEL PEACEFUL BECAUSE…

MY TRUTH STATEMENT IS…

MY DREAMS COMING TRUE LOOKS LIKE…
(CLOSE YOUR EYES AND VISUALIZE THIS 2-3 MINUTES, WRITING NOTES HERE IS OPTIONAL)

5 THINGS I'M GRATEFUL FOR TONIGHT (BE SPECIFIC)

_____

_____

_____

_____

_____

5 BIGGEST ACHIEVEMENTS OF MY LIFE (GOALS)

_____

_____

_____

_____

_____

5 EVALUATION FOR TODAY

DID I TAKE ACTION TOWARD MY FIRST GOAL TODAY, FOCUSED FOR AT LEAST 45 MINS?

_____

DID I KEEP TODAY'S PROMISE TO MYSELF? DID I WORKOUT OR MOVE TODAY?

_____

DID I REPRESENT WHO I AM BECOMING AND WANT TO BE TODAY?

_____

ONE THING I AM PROUD OF MYSELF FOR TODAY:

_____

ONE THING I CAN DO BETTER TOMORROW OR WHERE I CAN SHOW MORE LOVE:

_____

EVENING CHECKLIST

- ☐ CELL PHONE OFF 30 MINS BEFORE SLEEP
- ☐ TAKE 5 DEEP BREATHS
- ☐ 5-10 MINS READING OR JOURNALING
- ☐ SKIN CARE (CLEANSE, TONE, MOISTURIZE, SERUM)
- ☐ ORAL HYGEINE (BRUSH, FLOSS, MOUTHWASH)
- ☐ FULL BODY STRETCH
- ☐ PRAY OR MEDITATE
- ☐ EVENING SUPPLEMENTS OR ESSENTIAL OILS
- ☐ TURN ON DIFFUSER IN BEDROOM WITH CALMING OILS

I FEEL PEACEFUL BECAUSE…

MY TRUTH STATEMENT IS…

MY DREAMS COMING TRUE LOOKS LIKE…
(CLOSE YOUR EYES AND VISUALIZE THIS 2-3 MINUTES, WRITING NOTES HERE IS OPTIONAL)

5 THINGS I'M GRATEFUL FOR TONIGHT (BE SPECIFIC)

5 BIGGEST ACHIEVEMENTS OF MY LIFE (GOALS)

---

5 EVALUATION FOR TODAY

DID I TAKE ACTION TOWARD MY FIRST GOAL TODAY, FOCUSED FOR AT LEAST 45 MINS?

_____

DID I KEEP TODAY'S PROMISE TO MYSELF? DID I WORKOUT OR MOVE TODAY?

_____

DID I REPRESENT WHO I AM BECOMING AND WANT TO BE TODAY?

_____

ONE THING I AM PROUD OF MYSELF FOR TODAY:

_____

ONE THING I CAN DO BETTER TOMORROW OR WHERE I CAN SHOW MORE LOVE:

_____

EVENING CHECKLIST

- [ ] CELL PHONE OFF 30 MINS BEFORE SLEEP
- [ ] TAKE 5 DEEP BREATHS
- [ ] 5-10 MINS READING OR JOURNALING
- [ ] SKIN CARE (CLEANSE, TONE, MOISTURIZE, SERUM)
- [ ] ORAL HYGEINE (BRUSH, FLOSS, MOUTHWASH)
- [ ] FULL BODY STRETCH
- [ ] PRAY OR MEDITATE
- [ ] EVENING SUPPLEMENTS OR ESSENTIAL OILS
- [ ] TURN ON DIFFUSER IN BEDROOM WITH CALMING OILS

I FEEL PEACEFUL BECAUSE...

MY TRUTH STATEMENT IS...

MY DREAMS COMING TRUE LOOKS LIKE...
(CLOSE YOUR EYES AND VISUALIZE THIS 2-3 MINUTES, WRITING NOTES HERE IS OPTIONAL)

5 | THINGS I'M GRATEFUL FOR TONIGHT (BE SPECIFIC)

_____

_____

_____

_____

_____

5 | BIGGEST ACHIEVEMENTS OF MY LIFE (GOALS)

_____

_____

_____

_____

_____

5 | EVALUATION FOR TODAY

DID I TAKE ACTION TOWARD MY FIRST GOAL TODAY, FOCUSED FOR AT LEAST 45 MINS?

_____

DID I KEEP TODAY'S PROMISE TO MYSELF? DID I WORKOUT OR MOVE TODAY?

_____

DID I REPRESENT WHO I AM BECOMING AND WANT TO BE TODAY?

_____

ONE THING I AM PROUD OF MYSELF FOR TODAY:

_____

ONE THING I CAN DO BETTER TOMORROW OR WHERE I CAN SHOW MORE LOVE:

_____

EVENING CHECKLIST

- [ ] CELL PHONE OFF 30 MINS BEFORE SLEEP
- [ ] TAKE 5 DEEP BREATHS
- [ ] 5-10 MINS READING OR JOURNALING
- [ ] SKIN CARE (CLEANSE, TONE, MOISTURIZE, SERUM)
- [ ] ORAL HYGEINE (BRUSH, FLOSS, MOUTHWASH)
- [ ] FULL BODY STRETCH
- [ ] PRAY OR MEDITATE
- [ ] EVENING SUPPLEMENTS OR ESSENTIAL OILS
- [ ] TURN ON DIFFUSER IN BEDROOM WITH CALMING OILS

I FEEL PEACEFUL BECAUSE...

MY TRUTH STATEMENT IS...

MY DREAMS COMING TRUE LOOKS LIKE...
(CLOSE YOUR EYES AND VISUALIZE THIS 2-3 MINUTES, WRITING NOTES HERE IS OPTIONAL)

5 THINGS I'M GRATEFUL FOR
TONIGHT (BE SPECIFIC)

5 BIGGEST ACHIEVEMENTS
OF MY LIFE (GOALS)

_____

_____

_____

_____

_____

_____

_____

_____

_____

_____

5 EVALUATION FOR TODAY

DID I TAKE ACTION TOWARD MY FIRST GOAL TODAY, FOCUSED FOR AT LEAST 45 MINS?

_____

DID I KEEP TODAY'S PROMISE TO MYSELF? DID I WORKOUT OR MOVE TODAY?

_____

DID I REPRESENT WHO I AM BECOMING AND WANT TO BE TODAY?

_____

ONE THING I AM PROUD OF MYSELF FOR TODAY:

_____

ONE THING I CAN DO BETTER TOMORROW OR WHERE I CAN SHOW MORE LOVE:

_____

EVENING CHECKLIST

- ☐ CELL PHONE OFF 30 MINS BEFORE SLEEP
- ☐ TAKE 5 DEEP BREATHS
- ☐ 5-10 MINS READING OR JOURNALING
- ☐ SKIN CARE (CLEANSE, TONE, MOISTURIZE, SERUM)
- ☐ ORAL HYGEINE (BRUSH, FLOSS, MOUTHWASH)
- ☐ FULL BODY STRETCH
- ☐ PRAY OR MEDITATE
- ☐ EVENING SUPPLEMENTS OR ESSENTIAL OILS
- ☐ TURN ON DIFFUSER IN BEDROOM WITH CALMING OILS

I FEEL PEACEFUL BECAUSE…

MY TRUTH STATEMENT IS…

MY DREAMS COMING TRUE LOOKS LIKE…
(CLOSE YOUR EYES AND VISUALIZE THIS 2-3 MINUTES, WRITING NOTES HERE IS OPTIONAL)

5 THINGS I'M GRATEFUL FOR
TONIGHT (BE SPECIFIC)

5 BIGGEST ACHIEVEMENTS
OF MY LIFE (GOALS)

_____

_____

_____

_____

_____

_____

_____

_____

_____

_____

---

5 EVALUATION FOR TODAY

DID I TAKE ACTION TOWARD MY FIRST GOAL TODAY, FOCUSED FOR AT LEAST 45 MINS?

_____

DID I KEEP TODAY'S PROMISE TO MYSELF? DID I WORKOUT OR MOVE TODAY?

_____

DID I REPRESENT WHO I AM BECOMING AND WANT TO BE TODAY?

_____

ONE THING I AM PROUD OF MYSELF FOR TODAY:

_____

ONE THING I CAN DO BETTER TOMORROW OR WHERE I CAN SHOW MORE LOVE:

_____

EVENING CHECKLIST

- ☐ CELL PHONE OFF 30 MINS BEFORE SLEEP
- ☐ TAKE 5 DEEP BREATHS
- ☐ 5-10 MINS READING OR JOURNALING
- ☐ SKIN CARE (CLEANSE, TONE, MOISTURIZE, SERUM)
- ☐ ORAL HYGEINE (BRUSH, FLOSS, MOUTHWASH)
- ☐ FULL BODY STRETCH
- ☐ PRAY OR MEDITATE
- ☐ EVENING SUPPLEMENTS OR ESSENTIAL OILS
- ☐ TURN ON DIFFUSER IN BEDROOM WITH CALMING OILS

I FEEL PEACEFUL BECAUSE…

MY TRUTH STATEMENT IS…

MY DREAMS COMING TRUE LOOKS LIKE…
(CLOSE YOUR EYES AND VISUALIZE THIS 2-3 MINUTES, WRITING NOTES HERE IS OPTIONAL)

5 | THINGS I'M GRATEFUL FOR TONIGHT (BE SPECIFIC)

_____

_____

_____

_____

_____

5 | BIGGEST ACHIEVEMENTS OF MY LIFE (GOALS)

_____

_____

_____

_____

_____

5 | EVALUATION FOR TODAY

DID I TAKE ACTION TOWARD MY FIRST GOAL TODAY, FOCUSED FOR AT LEAST 45 MINS?

_____

DID I KEEP TODAY'S PROMISE TO MYSELF? DID I WORKOUT OR MOVE TODAY?

_____

DID I REPRESENT WHO I AM BECOMING AND WANT TO BE TODAY?

_____

ONE THING I AM PROUD OF MYSELF FOR TODAY:

_____

ONE THING I CAN DO BETTER TOMORROW OR WHERE I CAN SHOW MORE LOVE:

_____

EVENING CHECKLIST

- ☐ CELL PHONE OFF 30 MINS BEFORE SLEEP
- ☐ TAKE 5 DEEP BREATHS
- ☐ 5-10 MINS READING OR JOURNALING
- ☐ SKIN CARE (CLEANSE, TONE, MOISTURIZE, SERUM)
- ☐ ORAL HYGEINE (BRUSH, FLOSS, MOUTHWASH)
- ☐ FULL BODY STRETCH
- ☐ PRAY OR MEDITATE
- ☐ EVENING SUPPLEMENTS OR ESSENTIAL OILS
- ☐ TURN ON DIFFUSER IN BEDROOM WITH CALMING OILS

I FEEL PEACEFUL BECAUSE…

MY TRUTH STATEMENT IS…

MY DREAMS COMING TRUE LOOKS LIKE…
(CLOSE YOUR EYES AND VISUALIZE THIS 2-3 MINUTES, WRITING NOTES HERE IS OPTIONAL)

5 THINGS I'M GRATEFUL FOR TONIGHT (BE SPECIFIC)

_____

_____

_____

_____

_____

5 BIGGEST ACHIEVEMENTS OF MY LIFE (GOALS)

_____

_____

_____

_____

_____

5 EVALUATION FOR TODAY

DID I TAKE ACTION TOWARD MY FIRST GOAL TODAY, FOCUSED FOR AT LEAST 45 MINS?

_____

DID I KEEP TODAY'S PROMISE TO MYSELF? DID I WORKOUT OR MOVE TODAY?

_____

DID I REPRESENT WHO I AM BECOMING AND WANT TO BE TODAY?

_____

ONE THING I AM PROUD OF MYSELF FOR TODAY:

_____

ONE THING I CAN DO BETTER TOMORROW OR WHERE I CAN SHOW MORE LOVE:

_____

EVENING CHECKLIST

- ☐ CELL PHONE OFF 30 MINS BEFORE SLEEP
- ☐ TAKE 5 DEEP BREATHS
- ☐ 5-10 MINS READING OR JOURNALING
- ☐ SKIN CARE (CLEANSE, TONE, MOISTURIZE, SERUM)
- ☐ ORAL HYGEINE (BRUSH, FLOSS, MOUTHWASH)
- ☐ FULL BODY STRETCH
- ☐ PRAY OR MEDITATE
- ☐ EVENING SUPPLEMENTS OR ESSENTIAL OILS
- ☐ TURN ON DIFFUSER IN BEDROOM WITH CALMING OILS

I FEEL PEACEFUL BECAUSE...

MY TRUTH STATEMENT IS...

MY DREAMS COMING TRUE LOOKS LIKE...
(CLOSE YOUR EYES AND VISUALIZE THIS 2-3 MINUTES, WRITING NOTES HERE IS OPTIONAL)

5 THINGS I'M GRATEFUL FOR TONIGHT (BE SPECIFIC)

_____

_____

_____

_____

_____

5 BIGGEST ACHIEVEMENTS OF MY LIFE (GOALS)

_____

_____

_____

_____

_____

5 EVALUATION FOR TODAY

DID I TAKE ACTION TOWARD MY FIRST GOAL TODAY, FOCUSED FOR AT LEAST 45 MINS?

_____

DID I KEEP TODAY'S PROMISE TO MYSELF? DID I WORKOUT OR MOVE TODAY?

_____

DID I REPRESENT WHO I AM BECOMING AND WANT TO BE TODAY?

_____

ONE THING I AM PROUD OF MYSELF FOR TODAY:

_____

ONE THING I CAN DO BETTER TOMORROW OR WHERE I CAN SHOW MORE LOVE:

_____

EVENING CHECKLIST

- [ ] CELL PHONE OFF 30 MINS BEFORE SLEEP
- [ ] TAKE 5 DEEP BREATHS
- [ ] 5-10 MINS READING OR JOURNALING
- [ ] SKIN CARE (CLEANSE, TONE, MOISTURIZE, SERUM)
- [ ] ORAL HYGEINE (BRUSH, FLOSS, MOUTHWASH)
- [ ] FULL BODY STRETCH
- [ ] PRAY OR MEDITATE
- [ ] EVENING SUPPLEMENTS OR ESSENTIAL OILS
- [ ] TURN ON DIFFUSER IN BEDROOM WITH CALMING OILS

I FEEL PEACEFUL BECAUSE...

MY TRUTH STATEMENT IS...

MY DREAMS COMING TRUE LOOKS LIKE...
(CLOSE YOUR EYES AND VISUALIZE THIS 2-3 MINUTES, WRITING NOTES HERE IS OPTIONAL)

5 THINGS I'M GRATEFUL FOR TONIGHT (BE SPECIFIC)

_____

_____

_____

_____

_____

5 BIGGEST ACHIEVEMENTS OF MY LIFE (GOALS)

_____

_____

_____

_____

_____

5 EVALUATION FOR TODAY

DID I TAKE ACTION TOWARD MY FIRST GOAL TODAY, FOCUSED FOR AT LEAST 45 MINS?

_____

DID I KEEP TODAY'S PROMISE TO MYSELF? DID I WORKOUT OR MOVE TODAY?

_____

DID I REPRESENT WHO I AM BECOMING AND WANT TO BE TODAY?

_____

ONE THING I AM PROUD OF MYSELF FOR TODAY:

_____

ONE THING I CAN DO BETTER TOMORROW OR WHERE I CAN SHOW MORE LOVE:

_____

EVENING CHECKLIST

- [ ] CELL PHONE OFF 30 MINS BEFORE SLEEP
- [ ] TAKE 5 DEEP BREATHS
- [ ] 5-10 MINS READING OR JOURNALING
- [ ] SKIN CARE (CLEANSE, TONE, MOISTURIZE, SERUM)
- [ ] ORAL HYGEINE (BRUSH, FLOSS, MOUTHWASH)
- [ ] FULL BODY STRETCH
- [ ] PRAY OR MEDITATE
- [ ] EVENING SUPPLEMENTS OR ESSENTIAL OILS
- [ ] TURN ON DIFFUSER IN BEDROOM WITH CALMING OILS

I FEEL PEACEFUL BECAUSE…

MY TRUTH STATEMENT IS…

MY DREAMS COMING TRUE LOOKS LIKE…
(CLOSE YOUR EYES AND VISUALIZE THIS 2-3 MINUTES, WRITING NOTES HERE IS OPTIONAL)

5 THINGS I'M GRATEFUL FOR TONIGHT (BE SPECIFIC)

_____

_____

_____

_____

_____

5 BIGGEST ACHIEVEMENTS OF MY LIFE (GOALS)

_____

_____

_____

_____

_____

5 EVALUATION FOR TODAY

DID I TAKE ACTION TOWARD MY FIRST GOAL TODAY, FOCUSED FOR AT LEAST 45 MINS?

_____

DID I KEEP TODAY'S PROMISE TO MYSELF? DID I WORKOUT OR MOVE TODAY?

_____

DID I REPRESENT WHO I AM BECOMING AND WANT TO BE TODAY?

_____

ONE THING I AM PROUD OF MYSELF FOR TODAY:

_____

ONE THING I CAN DO BETTER TOMORROW OR WHERE I CAN SHOW MORE LOVE:

_____

EVENING CHECKLIST

- [ ] CELL PHONE OFF 30 MINS BEFORE SLEEP
- [ ] TAKE 5 DEEP BREATHS
- [ ] 5-10 MINS READING OR JOURNALING
- [ ] SKIN CARE (CLEANSE, TONE, MOISTURIZE, SERUM)
- [ ] ORAL HYGEINE (BRUSH, FLOSS, MOUTHWASH)
- [ ] FULL BODY STRETCH
- [ ] PRAY OR MEDITATE
- [ ] EVENING SUPPLEMENTS OR ESSENTIAL OILS
- [ ] TURN ON DIFFUSER IN BEDROOM WITH CALMING OILS

I FEEL PEACEFUL BECAUSE...

MY TRUTH STATEMENT IS...

MY DREAMS COMING TRUE LOOKS LIKE...
(CLOSE YOUR EYES AND VISUALIZE THIS 2-3 MINUTES, WRITING NOTES HERE IS OPTIONAL)

5 | THINGS I'M GRATEFUL FOR TONIGHT (BE SPECIFIC)

_____

_____

_____

_____

_____

5 | BIGGEST ACHIEVEMENTS OF MY LIFE (GOALS)

_____

_____

_____

_____

_____

5 | EVALUATION FOR TODAY

DID I TAKE ACTION TOWARD MY FIRST GOAL TODAY, FOCUSED FOR AT LEAST 45 MINS?

_____

DID I KEEP TODAY'S PROMISE TO MYSELF? DID I WORKOUT OR MOVE TODAY?

_____

DID I REPRESENT WHO I AM BECOMING AND WANT TO BE TODAY?

_____

ONE THING I AM PROUD OF MYSELF FOR TODAY:

_____

ONE THING I CAN DO BETTER TOMORROW OR WHERE I CAN SHOW MORE LOVE:

_____

EVENING CHECKLIST

- [ ] CELL PHONE OFF 30 MINS BEFORE SLEEP
- [ ] TAKE 5 DEEP BREATHS
- [ ] 5-10 MINS READING OR JOURNALING
- [ ] SKIN CARE (CLEANSE, TONE, MOISTURIZE, SERUM)
- [ ] ORAL HYGEINE (BRUSH, FLOSS, MOUTHWASH)
- [ ] FULL BODY STRETCH
- [ ] PRAY OR MEDITATE
- [ ] EVENING SUPPLEMENTS OR ESSENTIAL OILS
- [ ] TURN ON DIFFUSER IN BEDROOM WITH CALMING OILS

I FEEL PEACEFUL BECAUSE…

MY TRUTH STATEMENT IS…

MY DREAMS COMING TRUE LOOKS LIKE…
(CLOSE YOUR EYES AND VISUALIZE THIS 2-3 MINUTES, WRITING NOTES HERE IS OPTIONAL)

5 | THINGS I'M GRATEFUL FOR TONIGHT (BE SPECIFIC)

_____

_____

_____

_____

5 | BIGGEST ACHIEVEMENTS OF MY LIFE (GOALS)

_____

_____

_____

_____

5 | EVALUATION FOR TODAY

DID I TAKE ACTION TOWARD MY FIRST GOAL TODAY, FOCUSED FOR AT LEAST 45 MINS?

_____

DID I KEEP TODAY'S PROMISE TO MYSELF? DID I WORKOUT OR MOVE TODAY?

_____

DID I REPRESENT WHO I AM BECOMING AND WANT TO BE TODAY?

_____

ONE THING I AM PROUD OF MYSELF FOR TODAY:

_____

ONE THING I CAN DO BETTER TOMORROW OR WHERE I CAN SHOW MORE LOVE:

_____

EVENING CHECKLIST

- [ ] CELL PHONE OFF 30 MINS BEFORE SLEEP
- [ ] TAKE 5 DEEP BREATHS
- [ ] 5-10 MINS READING OR JOURNALING
- [ ] SKIN CARE (CLEANSE, TONE, MOISTURIZE, SERUM)
- [ ] ORAL HYGEINE (BRUSH, FLOSS, MOUTHWASH)
- [ ] FULL BODY STRETCH
- [ ] PRAY OR MEDITATE
- [ ] EVENING SUPPLEMENTS OR ESSENTIAL OILS
- [ ] TURN ON DIFFUSER IN BEDROOM WITH CALMING OILS

I FEEL PEACEFUL BECAUSE…

MY TRUTH STATEMENT IS…

MY DREAMS COMING TRUE LOOKS LIKE…
(CLOSE YOUR EYES AND VISUALIZE THIS 2-3 MINUTES, WRITING NOTES HERE IS OPTIONAL)

5 THINGS I'M GRATEFUL FOR TONIGHT (BE SPECIFIC)

_____

_____

_____

_____

_____

5 BIGGEST ACHIEVEMENTS OF MY LIFE (GOALS)

_____

_____

_____

_____

_____

5 EVALUATION FOR TODAY

DID I TAKE ACTION TOWARD MY FIRST GOAL TODAY, FOCUSED FOR AT LEAST 45 MINS?

_____

DID I KEEP TODAY'S PROMISE TO MYSELF? DID I WORKOUT OR MOVE TODAY?

_____

DID I REPRESENT WHO I AM BECOMING AND WANT TO BE TODAY?

_____

ONE THING I AM PROUD OF MYSELF FOR TODAY:

_____

ONE THING I CAN DO BETTER TOMORROW OR WHERE I CAN SHOW MORE LOVE:

_____

EVENING CHECKLIST

- ☐ CELL PHONE OFF 30 MINS BEFORE SLEEP
- ☐ TAKE 5 DEEP BREATHS
- ☐ 5-10 MINS READING OR JOURNALING
- ☐ SKIN CARE (CLEANSE, TONE, MOISTURIZE, SERUM)
- ☐ ORAL HYGEINE (BRUSH, FLOSS, MOUTHWASH)
- ☐ FULL BODY STRETCH
- ☐ PRAY OR MEDITATE
- ☐ EVENING SUPPLEMENTS OR ESSENTIAL OILS
- ☐ TURN ON DIFFUSER IN BEDROOM WITH CALMING OILS

I FEEL PEACEFUL BECAUSE…

MY TRUTH STATEMENT IS…

MY DREAMS COMING TRUE LOOKS LIKE…
(CLOSE YOUR EYES AND VISUALIZE THIS 2-3 MINUTES, WRITING NOTES HERE IS OPTIONAL)

5 | THINGS I'M GRATEFUL FOR TONIGHT (BE SPECIFIC)

_____

_____

_____

_____

_____

5 | BIGGEST ACHIEVEMENTS OF MY LIFE (GOALS)

_____

_____

_____

_____

_____

5 | EVALUATION FOR TODAY

DID I TAKE ACTION TOWARD MY FIRST GOAL TODAY, FOCUSED FOR AT LEAST 45 MINS?

_____

DID I KEEP TODAY'S PROMISE TO MYSELF? DID I WORKOUT OR MOVE TODAY?

_____

DID I REPRESENT WHO I AM BECOMING AND WANT TO BE TODAY?

_____

ONE THING I AM PROUD OF MYSELF FOR TODAY:

_____

ONE THING I CAN DO BETTER TOMORROW OR WHERE I CAN SHOW MORE LOVE:

_____

EVENING CHECKLIST

- ☐ CELL PHONE OFF 30 MINS BEFORE SLEEP
- ☐ TAKE 5 DEEP BREATHS
- ☐ 5-10 MINS READING OR JOURNALING
- ☐ SKIN CARE (CLEANSE, TONE, MOISTURIZE, SERUM)
- ☐ ORAL HYGEINE (BRUSH, FLOSS, MOUTHWASH)
- ☐ FULL BODY STRETCH
- ☐ PRAY OR MEDITATE
- ☐ EVENING SUPPLEMENTS OR ESSENTIAL OILS
- ☐ TURN ON DIFFUSER IN BEDROOM WITH CALMING OILS

I FEEL PEACEFUL BECAUSE…

MY TRUTH STATEMENT IS…

MY DREAMS COMING TRUE LOOKS LIKE…
(CLOSE YOUR EYES AND VISUALIZE THIS 2-3 MINUTES, WRITING NOTES HERE IS OPTIONAL)

5 THINGS I'M GRATEFUL FOR TONIGHT (BE SPECIFIC)

---

5 BIGGEST ACHIEVEMENTS OF MY LIFE (GOALS)

---

5 EVALUATION FOR TODAY

DID I TAKE ACTION TOWARD MY FIRST GOAL TODAY, FOCUSED FOR AT LEAST 45 MINS?

DID I KEEP TODAY'S PROMISE TO MYSELF? DID I WORKOUT OR MOVE TODAY?

DID I REPRESENT WHO I AM BECOMING AND WANT TO BE TODAY?

ONE THING I AM PROUD OF MYSELF FOR TODAY:

ONE THING I CAN DO BETTER TOMORROW OR WHERE I CAN SHOW MORE LOVE:

EVENING CHECKLIST

- ☐ CELL PHONE OFF 30 MINS BEFORE SLEEP
- ☐ TAKE 5 DEEP BREATHS
- ☐ 5-10 MINS READING OR JOURNALING
- ☐ SKIN CARE (CLEANSE, TONE, MOISTURIZE, SERUM)
- ☐ ORAL HYGEINE (BRUSH, FLOSS, MOUTHWASH)
- ☐ FULL BODY STRETCH
- ☐ PRAY OR MEDITATE
- ☐ EVENING SUPPLEMENTS OR ESSENTIAL OILS
- ☐ TURN ON DIFFUSER IN BEDROOM WITH CALMING OILS

I FEEL PEACEFUL BECAUSE…

MY TRUTH STATEMENT IS…

MY DREAMS COMING TRUE LOOKS LIKE…
(CLOSE YOUR EYES AND VISUALIZE THIS 2-3 MINUTES, WRITING NOTES HERE IS OPTIONAL)

Made in the USA
Monee, IL
20 May 2020